MINING ENGINEERING - RESEARCH AND TECHNOLOGY

URANIUM MINING AND MANAGEMENT

FEDERAL CONSIDERATIONS

Mining Engineering - Research and Technology

Additional books in this series can be found on Nova's website under the Series tab.

Additional e-books in this series can be found on Nova's website under the e-books tab.

Environmental Remediation Technologies, Regulations and Safety

Additional books in this series can be found on Nova's website under the Series tab.

Additional e-books in this series can be found on Nova's website under the e-books tab.

MINING ENGINEERING - RESEARCH AND TECHNOLOGY

URANIUM MINING AND MANAGEMENT

FEDERAL CONSIDERATIONS

JORDAN DUNN
AND
DWAYNE ARNOLD
EDITORS

New York

Copyright © 2012 by Nova Science Publishers, Inc.

All rights reserved. No part of this book may be reproduced, stored in a retrieval system or transmitted in any form or by any means: electronic, electrostatic, magnetic, tape, mechanical photocopying, recording or otherwise without the written permission of the Publisher.

For permission to use material from this book please contact us:
Telephone 631-231-7269; Fax 631-231-8175
Web Site: http://www.novapublishers.com

NOTICE TO THE READER

The Publisher has taken reasonable care in the preparation of this book, but makes no expressed or implied warranty of any kind and assumes no responsibility for any errors or omissions. No liability is assumed for incidental or consequential damages in connection with or arising out of information contained in this book. The Publisher shall not be liable for any special, consequential, or exemplary damages resulting, in whole or in part, from the readers' use of, or reliance upon, this material. Any parts of this book based on government reports are so indicated and copyright is claimed for those parts to the extent applicable to compilations of such works.

Independent verification should be sought for any data, advice or recommendations contained in this book. In addition, no responsibility is assumed by the publisher for any injury and/or damage to persons or property arising from any methods, products, instructions, ideas or otherwise contained in this publication.

This publication is designed to provide accurate and authoritative information with regard to the subject matter covered herein. It is sold with the clear understanding that the Publisher is not engaged in rendering legal or any other professional services. If legal or any other expert assistance is required, the services of a competent person should be sought. FROM A DECLARATION OF PARTICIPANTS JOINTLY ADOPTED BY A COMMITTEE OF THE AMERICAN BAR ASSOCIATION AND A COMMITTEE OF PUBLISHERS.

Additional color graphics may be available in the e-book version of this book.

LIBRARY OF CONGRESS CATALOGING-IN-PUBLICATION DATA

ISBN: 978-1-62257-412-4

Published by Nova Science Publishers, Inc. † New York

CONTENTS

Preface		vii
Chapter 1	Uranium Mining: Opportunities Exist to Improve Oversight of Financial Assurances *United States Government Accountability Office*	1
Chapter 2	Excess Uranium Inventories: Clarifying DOE's Disposition Options Could Help Avoid Further Legal Violations *United States Government Accountability Office*	61
Index		105

PREFACE

This book examines uranium mining and management in the United States with a focus on federal considerations. From 2005 to 2007, uranium prices increased from about $20 a pound to over $140 a pound, which led to renewed interest in uranium mining, both exploration and extraction, on federal land in the U.S. In early 2012, thousands of claims have been filed to explore for and potentially extract uranium on federal land. This increase in claims filed, has raised concerns about the potential impacts that an increased level of uranium exploration and extraction could have on the environment. During uranium extraction, the waste rock piles that are formed can introduce radionuclides (such as radium) and heavy metals (such as selenium and arsenic) into the environment. Before the mid-1970s, many mines on federal land, were abandoned without any reclamation, leaving a costly legacy of abandoned mines that pose potential health, safety, and environmental hazards.

Chapter 1 – From 2005 through 2007, uranium prices increased from about $20 a pound to over $140 a pound, leading to renewed interest in uranium mining on federal land. This interest has raised concerns about the potential impacts that more uranium operations could have on the environment. GAO was asked to (1) compare key agencies' oversight of uranium exploration and extraction operations on federal land, (2) determine the number and status of uranium operations on federal land, (3) identify the coverage and amounts of financial assurances for reclaiming current uranium operations on federal land, and (4) examine what is known about the number and location of abandoned uranium mine sites on federal land and their potential cleanup costs. GAO reviewed agency reports and regulations, surveyed relevant agency field staff on the status of these operations, and examined federal data on uranium operations, financial assurances, and abandoned uranium mine sites.

Chapter 2 - Uranium is a key component in the production of nuclear energy and nuclear weapons. The Department of Energy (DOE) manages the nation's surplus uranium, which is derived in part from former nuclear weapons production. In 2008, DOE published a uranium management plan that set a target for DOE uranium sales and transfers to avert harm to the domestic uranium industry. In 2009, DOE began using natural uranium to pay for cleanup work at a former uranium enrichment facility in Ohio, without having identified such transactions in its 2008 plan. As directed, GAO reviewed DOE's uranium management program. This report examines (1) DOE's uranium transactions and plans for future transactions, (2) the extent to which these transactions were consistent with DOE's uranium management plan, and (3) the extent to which these transactions were consistent with federal law. GAO reviewed transaction documents and contracts and interviewed knowledgeable DOE, contractor, and uranium industry officials and uranium market analysts.

In: Uranium Mining and Management
Editors: J. Dunn and D. Arnold

ISBN: 978-1-62257-412-4
© 2012 Nova Science Publishers, Inc.

Chapter 1

URANIUM MINING: OPPORTUNITIES EXIST TO IMPROVE OVERSIGHT OF FINANCIAL ASSURANCES[*]

United States Government Accountability Office

WHY GAO DID THIS STUDY

From 2005 through 2007, uranium prices increased from about $20 a pound to over $140 a pound, leading to renewed interest in uranium mining on federal land. This interest has raised concerns about the potential impacts that more uranium operations could have on the environment. GAO was asked to (1) compare key agencies' oversight of uranium exploration and extraction operations on federal land, (2) determine the number and status of uranium operations on federal land, (3) identify the coverage and amounts of financial assurances for reclaiming current uranium operations on federal land, and (4) examine what is known about the number and location of abandoned uranium mine sites on federal land and their potential cleanup costs. GAO reviewed agency reports and regulations, surveyed relevant agency field staff on the status of these operations, and examined federal data on uranium operations, financial assurances, and abandoned uranium mine sites.

---

[*] This is an edited, reformatted and augmented version of the Highlights of GAO-12-544, a report to the Ranking Member, Committee on Natural Resources, House of Representatives, dated May 2012.

WHAT GAO RECOMMENDS

GAO recommends, among other things, that federal agencies better coordinate their efforts when establishing financial assurances and develop a consistent definition for abandoned mine sites. The Departments of the Interior, Agriculture, and Energy, along with NRC and the Environmental Protection Agency (EPA), concurred with these recommendations. In addition, Interior and EPA provided technical comments, which GAO incorporated as appropriate.

WHAT GAO FOUND

The Bureau of Land Management (BLM), the Forest Service, and the Department of Energy (DOE) are the key agencies that oversee uranium exploration and extraction on federal land, but GAO identified three areas where their oversight processes differ. First, these agencies have different processes for notification of uranium exploration or extraction activities on federal land. Second, the agencies require operators to have in place financial assurances to cover the full estimated cost of reclaiming a uranium operation, but they differ in who estimates the value of the financial assurance and the frequency of their reviews of the assurances. Third, under existing authorities, DOE can collect royalties or rents for uranium extraction, but BLM and the Forest Service cannot. DOE has collected about $64 million in rents and royalties from its leasing program since the 1940s.

As of January 2012, a total of 221 uranium operations were on federally managed land, but only 7 were actively extracting uranium and all of these were on BLM land. An additional 29 uranium operations were awaiting federal approval. Of the 202 operations on BLM land, the majority were engaged in either reclamation or exploration activities, according to BLM field officials. In addition, 3 uranium operations were on Forest Service land, and 16 operations were on lease tracts that DOE manages, none of which were actively extracting uranium.

As of January 2012, BLM, the Forest Service, and DOE reported having $249.1 million in financial assurances, and these assurances were generally adequate to cover the estimated reclamation costs for uranium operations on federal land. Nearly all of these assurances ($247.6 million) were for authorized uranium operations on BLM-managed land, with the remaining

$1.5 million for authorized operations on Forest Service land and for DOE's lease tracts. BLM and the Nuclear Regulatory Commission (NRC), which is responsible for overseeing some aspects of uranium operations on federal land, do not coordinate efforts to establish and review financial assurances for in situ recovery operations, which use a series of wells to extract uranium. Such operations account for a large percentage of the total financial assurances held by the agencies.

Federal agencies do not have reliable data on the number and location of abandoned uranium mine sites on federal land or a definitive cost for their cleanup. There are likely thousands of abandoned uranium mine sites on federal land, but GAO identified significant limitations in agencies' data that make their databases generally unreliable. For example, these databases do not have complete data and do not use a consistent definition of an abandoned mine site. Agencies do not know how many sites will need cleanup, and they do not have information on the total cost to clean up these sites. Based on agencies' experiences with cleanup at some sites, cleanup costs could vary significantly from thousands to hundreds of millions of dollars, depending on site-specific conditions and the amount and type of work required at each site.

ABBREVIATIONS

AMSCM	Abandoned Mine-Site Cleanup Module
BLM	Bureau of Land Management
CERCLA	Comprehensive Environmental Response, Compensation, and Liability Act
DOE	Department of Energy
EIA	Energy Information Administration
EPA	Environmental Protection Agency
ISR	in situ recovery
MRDS	Mineral Resources Data System
NEPA	National Environmental Policy Act
NRC	Nuclear Regulatory Commission
UIC	underground injection control
USGS	U.S. Geological Survey

May 17, 2012

The Honorable Edward J. Markey
Ranking Member
Committee on Natural Resources
House of Representatives

Dear Mr. Markey:

From 2005 through 2007, uranium prices increased from about $20 a pound to over $140 a pound, which led to renewed interest in uranium mining—both exploration and extraction—on federal land in the United States. In early April 2012, prices were about $50 per pound, but thousands of claims have been filed to explore for and potentially extract uranium on federal land. This increase in claims filed—the first step in a potentially lengthy process to explore and extract uranium—has raised concerns about the potential impacts that an increased level of uranium exploration and extraction could have on the environment. For example, during uranium extraction, the waste rock piles that are formed can introduce radionuclides (such as radium) and heavy metals (such as selenium and arsenic) into the environment. Before the mid-1970s, many mines on federal land, including uranium mines, were abandoned without any reclamation, leaving a costly legacy of abandoned mines that pose potential health, safety, and environmental hazards. Some of these hazards include open or concealed mine openings, unstable mine structures, and toxic or radioactive materials. In 2008, we reported that from fiscal years 1998 to 2007, the federal government had spent billions to reclaim abandoned hardrock mines, which include uranium mines.[1]

To mitigate these potential health, safety, and environmental hazards, mining operators are responsible for addressing safety hazards and reclaiming the site after their operations have ceased.[2] Activities that address safety hazards can include installing gates over mine openings. Reclamation activities can include reapplication of topsoil, and reshaping and revegetation of disturbed soil areas; measures to control erosion, landslides, and water runoff; measures to isolate, remove, or control toxic materials; and rehabilitation of fisheries and wildlife habitat.[3] Operators are required to obtain financial assurances to cover estimated reclamation costs, and the federal government can use these assurances to pay for reclamation activities if the operator does not reclaim the site.[4] Our past work has raised concern about the adequacy of financial assurances to cover potential reclamation costs for hardrock mining operations, including uranium, on federal land.[5]

A number of federal agencies are involved in the oversight of uranium mining activities on federal land. The Department of the Interior's Bureau of Land Management (BLM) and the Department of Agriculture's Forest Service regulate mining on public domain lands under the General Mining Act of 1872 and other federal land management laws, including the Federal Land Policy Management Act of 1976. The Department of Energy (DOE) administers a uranium leasing program on land that has been withdrawn from the public domain under the Atomic Energy Act of 1954. In addition, the Nuclear Regulatory Commission (NRC) regulates a newer form of extraction, known as in situ recovery (ISR), as a form of uranium milling. The Environmental Protection Agency (EPA) oversees or participates in the remediation of some abandoned mines and sets environmental standards for certain sites.[6] Federal agencies may also work with state agencies in overseeing uranium activities. For example, federal agencies may share responsibilities with states for reviewing financial assurances.

You asked us to provide information on the status of uranium mining on federal land. Our objectives were to (1) compare BLM, the Forest Service, and DOE oversight of uranium exploration and extraction operations on federal land; (2) determine the number and status of uranium operations on federal land; (3) examine the coverage and amounts of financial assurances in place for reclaiming current uranium operations on federal land; and (4) examine what is known about the number and location of abandoned uranium mines on federal land and their potential cleanup costs.

To compare how BLM, the Forest Service, and DOE oversee uranium exploration and extraction operations on federal land, we reviewed these agencies' regulations and associated guidance and spoke with agency officials about their implementation of these regulations.[7] In addition, we reviewed NRC and EPA regulations that are relevant to uranium operations and spoke with officials from those agencies. We also reviewed memorandums of understanding among the agencies that delineate their coordination and cooperation in regulating uranium operations, and we spoke with state mining and environmental quality officials to discuss their coordination with federal agencies. To determine the number and status of uranium operations on federal land, we analyzed data from BLM's LR2000 database, which is used to collect and store information on BLM land and programs, including hardrock mining operations. In addition, we administered a web-based survey to all BLM field staff with responsibilities for uranium operations and asked them to provide the status of these operations. Because the Forest Service and DOE oversee fewer operations, we did not send them our web-based survey, but instead reviewed agency documents and interviewed staff from these agencies to determine the number and status of the operations that they oversee.

To examine the financial assurances in place for uranium operations on federal land, we analyzed data and available reports from BLM, the Forest Service, and DOE. We also interviewed officials from these agencies on the processes in place to review financial assurances. As part of this analysis, we examined whether the financial assurances in place were adequate to cover the estimated costs of reclamation; we did not determine whether the estimated costs of reclamation were sound. To learn about the number and location of abandoned uranium mines on federal land, we reviewed data and interviewed officials from BLM, the Forest Service, EPA, the National Park Service, and DOE, which are all involved in efforts to clean up abandoned uranium mines. To assess the reliability of these data, we reviewed documentation from these agencies on their data and interviewed officials involved in collecting and compiling these data. We determined that these data were not sufficiently reliable. Because these data were the only federal data available, we used them to discuss in general terms the potential number of abandoned mine sites, and we describe the limitations of these data. To describe the potential cleanup costs posed by these mines, we identified a series of key cleanup categories that we and agency officials believe are representative of the types of actions that may be required at an abandoned mine. These cleanup categories include actions to (1) address safety hazards, (2) conduct surface reclamation, and (3) remediate environmental hazards.[8] Cleaning up an abandoned mine may involve work that falls across several of these cleanup categories. To provide a range of potential costs for such cleanup work, we asked federal officials for information on past work done to clean up abandoned uranium mines or, if no past work was available, we asked for detailed estimates. We conducted this performance audit from June 2011 through May 2012 in accordance with generally accepted government auditing standards. Those standards require that we plan and perform the audit to obtain sufficient, appropriate evidence to provide a reasonable basis for our findings and conclusions based on our audit objectives. We believe that the evidence obtained provides a reasonable basis for our findings and conclusions based on our audit objectives. A more detailed description of our scope and methodology is presented in appendix I.

BACKGROUND

Uranium is a hardrock mineral, and most U.S. uranium deposits are located in the western half of the United States, specifically in the states of Arizona, Colorado, New Mexico, Texas, Utah, and Wyoming.[9] In the United States, uranium has been primarily used as a fuel for electric power generation and for nuclear weapons. In 2010, U.S. uranium mines extracted 4.2 million pounds of uranium, 2 percent more than in 2009, according to DOE's Energy Information Administration (EIA).[10] However, domestic production of uranium is not sufficient to meet domestic demand, and the United States imports over 90 percent of its uranium from countries such as Australia, Canada, and Russia.

Hardrock mining operations consist of four primary stages—exploration, extraction, mineral processing, and reclamation. Several of these stages can take place simultaneously, depending on the characteristics of the operation. Exploration involves prospecting and other steps, such as drilling, to locate mineral deposits. Extraction generally entails developing the mining infrastructure (power, buildings, and roads) needed for extraction, as well as drilling, blasting, and hauling ore from mining areas to processing areas. During processing, operators crush or grind the ore and apply chemical treatments to extract the minerals of value. The material left after the minerals are extracted—waste rock or tailings (a combination of fluid and rock particles)—is then disposed of, often in a nearby pile or tailings pond. As described earlier, reclamation activities can include reshaping and revegetating disturbed areas; measures to control erosion; and measures to isolate, remove, or control toxic materials. While uranium mining operations are similar to other hardrock mining operations in environmental concerns, the wastes produced require additional environmental controls. Of particular concern is the presence of the natural by-products of uranium radioactive decay, most notably radium and the radioactive gas radon, as well as heavy metals, such as arsenic. All of these byproducts can pose a serious risk to human health or the environment, especially if they migrate to surface or ground water, or enter the environment after transforming into dust.

Uranium is extracted using one of three processes—underground mining, open pit mining, or ISR. Open pit and underground mining are generally considered conventional uranium extraction processes. In these processes, uranium ore is removed from the ground and is sent to an off-site processing acility, called a mill, where extracted uranium is concentrated into a product called yellowcake (U_3O_8).[11] The optimum extraction process is determined by the size, grade, depth, and geology of an ore body. Open pit mining is generally used for ore deposits relatively close to the surface, while underground mining is generally used for deeper deposits, as shown in figure 1. Open pit mining generally involves more surface disturbance than underground mining, and the amount of waste rock removed to reach the mineral is greater. Since the early 1960s until recently, most uranium has been extracted by using conventional extraction processes.

Unlike conventional extraction processes, ISR, a mining technique established in the 1970s and anticipated to become more widely used by the industry in the future, aims to extract uranium with less surface disturbance. ISR extracts uranium by injecting oxygenated water and carbon dioxide or sodium bicarbonate hundreds of feet underground to dissolve uranium located in a subsurface ore body contained within a layer of sedimentary rock. Once dissolved, the water and uranium mixture is pumped to the surface, where the uranium is captured on ion exchange resins, which are taken to a central facility to be processed into yellowcake. (See figure 2.) ISR operations typically involve several wellfields, which are composed of many injection and production wells, and these wellfields can spread over hundreds or thousands of acres, with monitoring wells at periodic intervals above, below, and surrounding the aquifer to monitor for groundwater contamination outside the aquifer. According to industry and government documents, ISR is gaining favor as the approach to extract uranium because it is a more cost-efficient method for recovering uranium ore that causes less surface disturbance and is safer for worker health.[12] The primary risk associated with ISR operations is the potential for contamination of nearby groundwater. When ISR operations cease, the groundwater is restored by removing and stabilizing hazardous metals, such as arsenic and selenium, which may have been disturbed by the operations, and all the wells are plugged. Experts currently do not agree on how long it will take to restore a wellfield after production ceases, or if full restoration is achievable. In a 2009 report on groundwater restoration efforts for 22 ISR wellfields on private land in Texas, the U.S. Geological Survey (USGS) found that it was difficult for these operations to restore groundwater to baseline values for heavy metals, such as uranium and selenium.[13] Specifically, USGS reported that measured levels of uranium and selenium increased following restoration efforts in the majority of the wellfields when compared with baseline values.

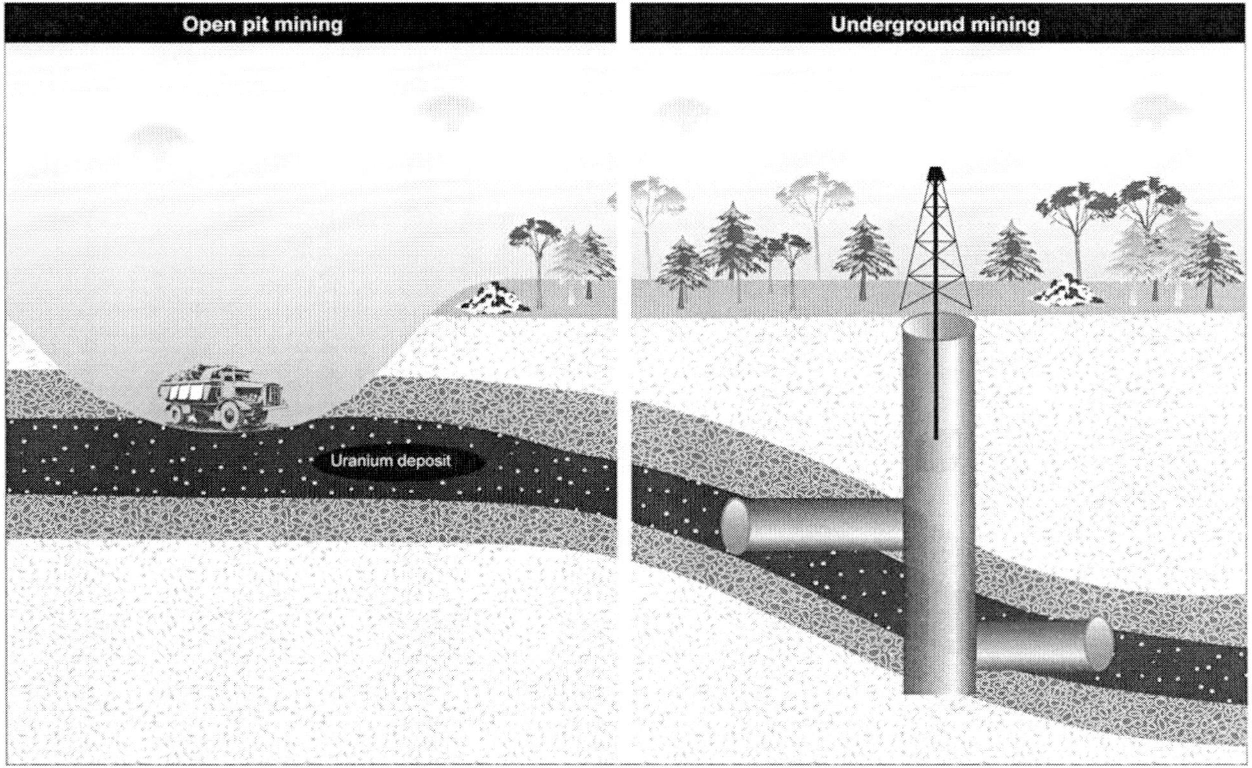

Sources: GAO analysis of information from EPA; Art Explosion (clip art).

Figure 1. Open Pit and Underground Uranium Mining.

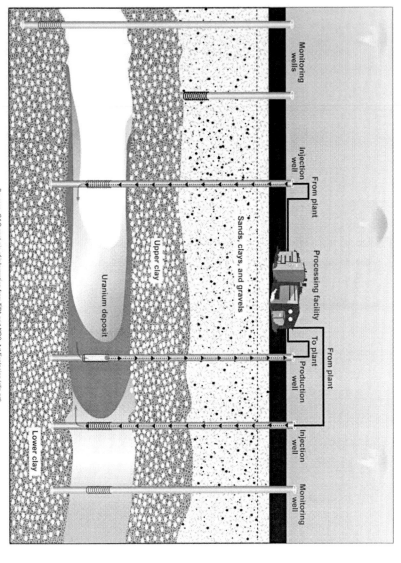

Figure 2. ISR Extraction Process for Uranium.

Three federal agencies play key roles in overseeing uranium operations on federal land: BLM, the Forest Service, and DOE. In addition, NRC, EPA, and the states are responsible for some aspects of uranium operations on federal, state, and private land.

- *BLM.* BLM manages more than 260 million acres of public lands located primarily in the western half of the United States. Under the General Mining Act of 1872 (Mining Act), an individual or corporation can establish a claim to any hardrock mineral on public land and may remove all hardrock minerals from the site. Under the Federal Land Policy and Management Act of 1976, BLM has developed and revised regulations and issued policies to prevent unnecessary or undue degradation of BLM land from hardrock operations. BLM issued regulations that took effect in 1981 that classified hardrock operations into three categories—casual use, notice-level operations, and plan-level operations—and required reclamation of the sites at the earliest feasible time. BLM issued revised regulations that took effect in 2001, to strengthen financial assurance requirements and modify the reclamation requirements, among other things. BLM delegates primary responsibility for oversight of hardrock operations to its state and local field offices.
- *The Forest Service.* The Forest Service manages approximately 193 million acres of national forests and grasslands throughout the United States. Forest Service regulations, promulgated under its Organic Act of 1897, among other laws, establish rules and procedures intended to ensure that hardrock mining operations minimize adverse environmental impacts on National Forest System surface resources. Since 1974, the Forest Service has required financial assurances for mining operations on National Forest System land. The Forest Service manages hardrock operations through its headquarters, 9 regions, 155 national forests and grasslands, and more than 600 ranger districts.
- *DOE.* DOE manages a uranium leasing program on 31 lease tracts, of which 29 are currently leased, under the authority of the Atomic Energy Act of 1954 (as amended).[14] These lease tracts cover about 25,000 acres of land located within the Uravan Mineral Belt in southwestern Colorado. These leases generally cover a period of 10 years, and DOE offers these leases through a competitive public bid solicitation, which specifies the lease terms, including the minimum annual royalties to be collected. DOE awards these leases to those

operators who offer to pay the highest royalty rate, who become known as lessees. This program began in 1948, when BLM withdrew certain uranium-rich land from the public domain, and reserved them for the use of DOE's predecessor agency, the Atomic Energy Commission, to secure and develop a supply of domestic uranium for the nation's defense needs. DOE manages mining activities, including exploration and extraction, associated with uranium and vanadium mining on these lands.[15] In 2005, DOE considered an expansion of the program in the face of increased demand for uranium, and initiated an environmental assessment of the program under the National Environmental Policy Act of 1969 (NEPA). DOE subsequently issued a finding that the expansion would have no significant impact on the environment. Environmental groups challenged this finding, and in 2011 a federal court prohibited further work on the leases as well as the issuance of new leases pending completion of a new environmental analysis.[16] DOE is in the process of developing a draft Programmatic Environmental Impact Statement that is expected to be released for public comment in late 2012. According to DOE documents, the lease program has approximately 13.5 million pounds of uranium left to mine.

- *NRC.* NRC is responsible for overseeing uranium milling operations, which produce yellowcake from uranium ore. ISR is considered a uranium milling operation by NRC because it produces yellowcake. NRC reviews ISR license applications, conducts environmental analyses and inspections, reviews decommissioning plans and activities, and oversees site reclamation and groundwater treatment. NRC can relinquish its regulatory authority to a state if the state and NRC determine that the state has a program that is adequate to protect public health and safety. NRC licenses and oversees ISR operations in Nebraska, New Mexico, and Wyoming, while the other states with major uranium deposits—Colorado, Texas, and Utah—license and oversee operations in their states.
- *EPA and the states.* EPA and the states also have a role in overseeing some aspects of uranium operations. Under the Clean Water Act, for example, EPA or the states issue permits to control pollutants that are discharged into the waters of the United States.[17] Under the Safe Drinking Water Act, the Underground Injection Control (UIC) program is designed to protect underground sources of drinking water by prohibiting the injection of fluids beneath the surface without a

permit.[18] Specifically, ISR operations require a class III UIC permit for wells because they inject fluids to dissolve and extract uranium. Class III wells must be constructed of appropriate materials to handle the fluid being injected and must be monitored during operations. When injection activities are complete, the injection wells must be plugged. In addition, under the Superfund program, established by the Comprehensive Environmental Response, Compensation, and Liability Act (CERCLA) of 1980, EPA, or, in some instances, other federal agencies if the contamination is on their land, has the authority to compel parties responsible for contaminating sites to clean them up or to clean the sites up itself and seek reimbursement. EPA places some of the most contaminated sites on the National Priority List, and resources from a federal trust fund, the Superfund, are available to pay for long-term cleanup at these sites. In addition, under the Uranium Mill Tailings Radiation Control Act, EPA has established standards for control of radioactive contamination to soil, air, and groundwater at certain uranium processing sites.[19] NRC regulations make EPA's groundwater protection standards generally applicable to uranium milling sites, including ISR operations.

States may play additional roles in regulating uranium operations on federal land. In general, states may have their own requirements governing the review of mining plans, environmental performance standards, reclamation, financial assurances, and inspection. For example, many states with uranium deposits require that an operator provide a financial assurance for the full cost of reclamation for a mining site.[20] Memorandums of understanding among the federal and state agencies aim to encourage coordination between states and federal agencies in overseeing mining operations.

Federal agencies must also comply with NEPA. NEPA requires federal agencies to analyze the likely environmental effects of proposed projects, which may include uranium mines, using an environmental assessment or, if the projects would likely significantly affect the environment, a more detailed environmental impact statement evaluating the proposed project and alternatives. An environmental impact statement results in a record of decision that lays out how anticipated environmental impacts will be mitigated.

AGENCIES DIFFER IN THEIR OVERSIGHT OF URANIUM OPERATIONS ON FEDERAL LAND

BLM, the Forest Service, and DOE all oversee uranium exploration and extraction operations on the federal land they manage, but we identified three areas where their processes differ: (1) notification of exploration or extraction operations, (2) oversight of financial assurances, and (3) royalties and rents earned.

BLM, the Forest Service, and DOE Have Different Processes for Notification of Exploration or Extraction

BLM, the Forest Service, and DOE require uranium operators to provide notification of their intent to undertake either uranium exploration or extraction activities on federal land, but their notification processes differ slightly. Under regulations for proposed activities on BLM land, "casual use"—generally defined as activities ordinarily resulting in no or negligible disturbance to the public lands or resources—is allowed without any notice.[21] For operations that are greater than casual use but that will disturb 5 acres or less of land, operators are required to file a notice with the local BLM field office 15 days before commencing operations. Under the regulations, BLM has 15 days to review the notice for completeness. To be complete, a notice must contain specified operator information, a sufficient description and schedule of the activity, a reclamation plan, and a reclamation cost estimate, among other information. Once a financial assurance is in place, the operator may begin operations once it hears from BLM that the notice is complete, or if it receives no word from BLM after 15 days. According to BLM guidance, the agency does not approve a notice and therefore is not required to perform an environmental review under NEPA for a notice.

Operations that constitute more than notice-level surface disturbance must submit a plan of operations to the local BLM field office for review and approval, according to BLM regulations. A plan of operations must include, among other information, specific operator information, a description and schedule of operations, a reclamation plan, a monitoring plan, and a reclamation cost estimate. BLM will review the plan within 30 days and then inform the operator that the plan is complete, that more information is required, or that additional steps must be completed. Upon completion of

BLM's review of the plan, including analysis under NEPA and public comment, BLM will notify the operator that it approves the plan, approves the plan subject to additional changes or conditions, or that it disapproves or withholds approval of the plan. Since 2001, BLM has been working on a draft handbook to guide its state and local field offices when reviewing notices and plans of operations. In the interim, BLM has issued a series of Instruction Memorandums to its field staff as guidance.

Like BLM, the Forest Service requires operators to provide notification of uranium operations, but the Forest Service differs in the activities it will allow under a notice of intent and plan of operations. Under Forest Service regulations, no notice is required for certain activity, such as collection of mineral specimens using hand tools, but a notice of intent is required for operations that might cause significant disturbance of surface resources, and a plan of operations is required for operations that will likely cause such a disturbance, such as use of mechanized equipment like a backhoe.[22] These standards apply regardless of the acreage involved. Forest Service officials told us that district forest rangers take the lead in reviewing and approving notice- and plan-level operations on Forest Service lands. The Forest Service does not perform environmental analysis under NEPA for projects that are not likely to cause significant disturbance, such as under a notice of intent. A NEPA environmental analysis is initiated only for plan-level operations, because they are more likely to cause significant disturbance.

DOE's notification requirements for its lease tracts differ from BLM's and the Forest Service's. DOE officials told us that the majority of its requirements for uranium operations are contained in its bid solicitation and in the terms of the lease, which incorporate relevant sections of DOE regulations. DOE notification requirements for exploration and extraction on its lease tracts are not contained in federal regulations. Instead, our review of two DOE lease documents showed that they contained a section specifying that the operator submit an exploration plan before beginning any surface disturbance to explore, test, or prospect for minerals. Furthermore, the leases specify that before developing a mine, a lessee must submit a separate mining plan to DOE for approval. DOE officials told us that because they oversee operations through a lease, they consider their role to be more like that of a landlord than a regulator. Under a DOE-BLM memorandum of understanding executed in April 2010, DOE has sole authority over the selection of lessees and the negotiation, issuance, management, and termination of leases. However, BLM has jurisdictional authority over all other surface and subsurface uses of the lease tracts and will review and provide comments on lessee plans as they relate to compliance with BLM regulations. According to DOE, it assesses specific tracts through the use of an environmental checklist; however, a more detailed environmental assessment may also take place. DOE reviews mining plans for consistency with its 2007 programmatic environmental assessment and existing environmental regulations.[23] Table 1 describes some of the differences in notification requirements among BLM, the Forest Service, and DOE.

BLM, the Forest Service, and DOE Differ in Their Oversight of Financial Assurances

BLM, the Forest Service, and DOE require operators to have financial assurances in place to cover the full estimated cost of reclaiming areas disturbed by operations; however, the agencies differ in who is responsible for initial calculation of these assurances, how frequently they conduct their review, how the review is documented, and how soon reclamation must begin after operations cease. (See table 2 for a summary of financial assurance requirements for the three agencies.) The full estimated cost to reclaim a site is typically defined as the sum sufficient for a third-party contractor to perform all necessary work, including measures to save topsoil for later reuse, control erosion, recontour the area disturbed, and revegetate or reseed the disturbed land. The estimate may also include agency administrative costs.

Table 1. Summary of Notification Requirements for Uranium Operations across Three Agencies

Agency	Filing requirement for a notice-level operation	Filing requirement for a plan of operations
BLM	Exploration-related surface disturbance of 5 acres or less	Exploration that disturbs more than 5 acres or any extraction-related operations
Forest Service	Operations that might cause significant disturbance of surface resources	Operations that are likely to cause significant disturbance of surface resources
DOE	Any exploration activity in keeping with terms of lease	Any extraction activity in keeping with terms of lease

Source: GAO analysis of information from BLM, the Forest Service, and DOE.

BLM regulations require operators to reclaim land disturbed by uranium operations. To ensure that this work is performed, since 2001, BLM has required the operator to provide a financial assurance. Operators must develop an estimate of the amount of financial assurance needed, which BLM reviews and adjusts as necessary. BLM does not have a minimum sum for a financial assurance. BLM uses its Bond Review Report to determine if the estimated costs of reclamation are adequate for ongoing operations, to take action to increase or decrease the financial assurance accordingly, and to certify that financial assurances are adequate to cover estimated reclamation costs. The Bond Review Report aggregates data from BLM's LR2000 database and includes data on the amount of financial assurances and when they were last reviewed. A BLM instruction memorandum directs local field offices to review financial assurances for adequacy every 2 years for notices and every 3 years for plans of operations.[24] In addition, by December 1 of each year, state BLM offices must review the Bond Review Report to determine if reclamation cost estimates for notices and plans of operations within their states are adequate and were reviewed within appropriate time frames. If the Bond Review Report indicates that a financial assurance is not adequate to cover estimated reclamation costs at a site or has not been reviewed within the appropriate time frame, then the state director must develop a corrective action plan to address the deficiencies. Following the end of operations at a site or when a notice expires, BLM regulations require reclamation of a notice to begin promptly, and reclamation of a plan of operations to begin at the earliest feasible time. Because BLM does not have an official definition for these time frames, BLM officials told us that local field offices have flexibility in determining whether operators are in compliance. Before a financial assurance is released back to the operator, the state agency responsible for mine permitting and the BLM local field office will inspect the site to verify that reclamation is complete. In some cases, reclamation can take several years, and a financial assurance may be reduced periodically before being released fully. Because many operations may involve a mix of federal, state, county, and private lands, BLM regulations provide the option of joint bonding with the state.[25] In these cases, the state holds the financial assurance, but it is also redeemable by BLM.

The Forest Service also directs operators to provide a financial assurance for the full cost of reclamation.[26] However, in contrast to BLM, the Forest Service relies on its technical staff at the district, forest, or regional level, not the operator, to calculate the estimated reclamation costs. It uses formal agency guidance issued in 2004 to calculate the estimated reclamation costs and proposes the amount of the financial assurance to cover those costs to the operator. The Forest Service does not have a required minimum for financial assurances on its lands. According to Forest Service guidance, an operator's financial assurances should be reviewed annually for adequacy, but a Forest Service official told us that agency staff do not prepare an annual report documenting these reviews. Forest Service regulations require that site reclamation begin upon exhaustion of the mineral deposit, at the earliest practicable time during operations, or within 1 year of the conclusion of operations, unless a longer time is allowed by the Forest Service. Forest Service and state officials will inspect a site to ensure that reclamation is complete before releasing the financial assurance. A financial assurance may also be released in increments as reclamation progresses. In most cases, the Forest Service holds the financial assurances for mining operations on its land, although a Forest Service official told us that the financial assurance could be jointly held with the state for larger operations.

Table 2. Summary of Financial Assurance Requirements for Uranium Operations across Three Agencies

Agency	Coverage required	Party responsible for initial calculation	Frequency of review	Documentation of review	When reclamation must begin following end of operations
BLM	Full cost of reclamation	Operator	24 months for a notice; 36 months for plan of operations	Documented in LR2000 and summarized annually in Bond Review Report	Promptly for notices; earliest feasible time for plans of operations
Forest Service	Full cost of reclamation	Forest Service	Annually	Recorded in case file, but no agencywide summary of review	Within 1 year, or longer with Forest Service approval
DOE	Full cost of reclamation	DOE	Periodically, or whenever lessee proposes a change in operations	Recorded in case file, but no agencywide summary of review	Promptly and must be completed within 180 days or date agreed to by DOE and lessee

Source: GAO analysis of information from BLM, the Forest Service, and DOE.

DOE also directs its personnel to ensure that the financial assurance provided by an operator is adequate to cover the estimated cost of reclamation. Sample lease agreements that we reviewed set a minimum financial assurance amount and state that DOE personnel will take into account estimated reclamation costs in setting the financial assurance. Similar to the Forest Service, DOE generally calculates this as the estimated amount for a third-party contractor to perform the reclamation work. The current minimum sum for DOE financial assurances is $5,000, according to DOE officials. Generally, DOE will perform a financial assurance assessment whenever the lessee puts forth new plans for a mining operation. The financial assurance review is filed in the case file as part of the approval package. Upon expiration of the lease, or early relinquishment or cancellation of the lease, current DOE lease terms require lessees to return the site to a condition satisfactory to DOE within 180 days, or a term otherwise agreed to by DOE and the lessee. DOE guidance states that DOE will release the financial assurance once the lessee's reclamation effort is deemed acceptable. Financial assurances are usually held by DOE, except in cases where disturbance to a DOE lease tract is minimal as part of a larger project undertaken on private or state lands.

Unlike BLM and the Forest Service, DOE Earns Royalties and Rents from Uranium Operations

Under existing statutory authorities, BLM and the Forest Service cannot collect rents for the use of federal land or charge royalties on hardrock minerals, including uranium, extracted from that land.[27] BLM does charge claimants an initial $34 location fee, a $15 processing fee, and an annual $140 maintenance fee per claim, and also collects these fees for claims on Forest Service land. In contrast, under the Atomic Energy Act, DOE may collect royalties and rents for uranium extraction operations on its lease tracts. DOE establishes the royalties and terms of payment with the lessee in the lease; typically potential lessees will offer to pay higher production royalties for lease tracts known to contain higher grades of uranium.[28]

DOE has collected approximately $64 million in royalties since the beginning of the lease program in the 1940s. Specifically:

- From the first round of leasing, 1949 through 1962, the program generated $5.9 million in royalties to the federal government from 1.2 million pounds of uranium and 6.8 million pounds of vanadium.

- From the second round of leasing, 1974 through 1994, the program generated $53 million in royalties for the federal government from production of approximately 6.5 million pounds of uranium and 33.4 million pounds of vanadium.
- From the third round of production, 2003 through 2005, the program generated $4.77 million in royalties for the federal government from production of approximately 390,000 pounds of uranium and 1.4 million pounds of vanadium.

In addition, current DOE leases require lessees to pay an annual rent. According to the program's annual status report, five companies collectively paid an annual rent of $387,040 in fiscal year 2010. Each lessee pays an amount according to the size and value of its lease tract. In lieu of paying this rent, DOE also allows lessees to perform reclamation work on previously abandoned mine sites. In fiscal year 2010, three companies negotiated with DOE to perform reclamation work in lieu of paying rent valued at a total of $101,860.

OVER 200 URANIUM OPERATIONS ARE ON FEDERAL LAND, BUT FEW ARE ACTIVELY EXTRACTING URANIUM

As of January 2012, a total of 221 uranium operations were on federally managed land, but only 7 of these operations were actively extracting uranium and these were all on BLM land.[29] An additional 29 uranium operations were awaiting federal approval. Most of the operations—202—were on BLM land; another 3 were on Forest Service land, and the remaining 16 were on DOE lease tracts.

Uranium Operations on BLM Land Are Generally Engaged in Exploration or Reclamation

Of the 221 uranium operations on federal land, 202, or 91 percent, were on land managed by BLM, according to our analysis of agency data. Of these 202 operations, BLM's LR2000 database identified 144 as authorized, which means BLM has acknowledged an operator's notice or has approved its plan of operations and has approved a financial assurance. These 144 operations included 111 notices and 33 plans of operations, covering about 13,400 acres, and were primarily located in Arizona, Colorado, Utah, and Wyoming. The remaining 58 operations on BLM land were expired notices—that is, operations have ceased except for reclamation and the financial assurance is held until BLM determines that reclamation is complete. According to our analysis of LR2000 data, we also identified 28 uranium operations (11 notices and 17 plans of operations) that were awaiting BLM's authorization. Collectively, these pending operations could involve disturbing up to 24,300 acres of BLM-managed land.[30]

We surveyed BLM staff in 25 field offices across eight states for additional information on the status of the uranium operations on BLM-managed land. As shown in table 3, we asked them to provide information on how many operations were in each of eight possible status categories. (For a more detailed description of the status categories that we used in our survey, please see app. I.) Specifically, on the basis of our survey responses, we determined the following:[31]

- Of the 144 authorized operations, 7 operations are actively extracting uranium—3 mines in Utah, 3 in Wyoming, and 1 in Arizona. In addition, 60 operations are engaged in exploration, 51 operations are engaged in reclamation, and 22 are on standby—that is, they are not actively exploring or extracting uranium.[32]
- Of the 58 expired operations, 40 are engaged in reclamation, and BLM staff did not know the status for 12 operations, in part because several of these operations had last been inspected in 2002. Most of the remaining 6 are either in standby or closed status.
- Of the 28 operations identified in LR2000 as pending, field staff reported a status for 12 operations that is inconsistent with BLMs definition of "pending." For example, staff reported 2 pending operations in exploration status, 4 pending operations in reclamation status, 3 pending operations in standby status, and 3 that were closed. Seventeen operations listed as pending in LR2000 were reported by field staff to be in a status that is consistent with the definition of pending, specifically exploration permitting or extraction permitting.

In addition, our review of documents for 110 of these operations confirmed that some of the reported status levels in LR2000 were inaccurate. For example, we found one notice that was denied in March 2007 that was still listed as pending in LR2000 as of January 2012. In another instance, a notice was authorized in October 2011 but was still listed in LR2000 as pending. There were other instances where the documentation that staff provided to us, such as inspection reports, had not been entered into LR2000. BLM guidance requires that field staff update LR2000 within 5 working days of a change in the status of the operation. Such delays in entering information affect the ability of LR2000 to serve as an effective management tool to track operations. According to the standards for internal control in the federal government, agencies are to promptly record transactions and events to maintain their relevance to management in controlling operations and making decisions.[33]

Table 3. Results of GAO's Survey of BLM Field Offices on Status of Uranium Operations

Type of operation	Exploration permitting	Exploration	Extraction permitting[a]	Extraction[a]	Standby	Reclamation	Closed	Other	Don't know
Authorized operations									
Authorized notices	1	55	0	0	7	45	5	2	0
Authorized plans of operations	1	5	2	7	15	6	0	1	0
Subtotal-authorized	2	60	2	7	22	51	5	3	0
Expired operations									
Expired notices	0	0	0	0	1	40	2	3	12
Pending operations									
Pending notices	2	1	0	0	1	4	2	2	0
Pending plans of operations	2	1	13	0	2	0	1	1	0
Subtotal-pending	4	2[b]	13	0	3[b]	4[b]	3[b]	3	0
Total	6	62	15	7	26	95	10	9	12

Source: GAO analysis of BLM field office responses.

Notes: Because an operation could have more than one status, field offices were allowed to select multiple status categories on our survey. As a result, the sum of the responses will exceed the total number of operations. Of the 230 operations, 9 were described by field staff using multiple statuses.

[a] On our survey, we used the terms "mine permitting" and "production." For the purposes of using consistent terms in this report, we are substituting the terms "extraction permitting" and "extraction."

[b] The status reported for these pending operations is inconsistent with BLM's definition of a pending operation.

Table 4. Summary of Operations That Are Extracting Uranium on BLM Land

Operation name	Operator	State	Type of mine
Arizona 1	Denison	Arizona	Underground
Daneros	Utah Energy	Utah	Underground
Pandora[a]	Denison	Utah	Underground
La Sal[a]	Denison	Utah	Underground
Highland[b]	Cameco	Wyoming	ISR
Smith Ranch[b]	Cameco	Wyoming	ISR
Willow Creek	Uranium One	Wyoming	ISR

Source: GAO analysis of BLM data, survey responses, and relevant BLM and company documents.

[a] Both the La Sal and Pandora mines are part of the La Sal Mine complex. We list them separately because they each have separate plans of operations with BLM. The plan of operations for the La Sal mine also includes the Beaver Shaft and Snowball mines. The Pandora mine includes some surface disturbance on Forest Service land resulting from the installation of a few vent holes for the mine; according to Forest Service officials, BLM is the primary federal agency involved in regulating this mine.

[b] The Smith Ranch and Highland operations are adjacent to each other and share a uranium processing facility. We list them separately because they have separate plans of operations with BLM.

Of the 7 operations actively extracting uranium on BLM-managed land, 4 are underground mines and 3 are ISR operations. See table 4 for more information on these operations. BLM officials told us the agency did not have data on how much uranium these operations were extracting because it is not authorized to collect this information on uranium or other hardrock minerals.

Three Uranium Operations Are on Forest Service Land

We identified three uranium operations on land managed by the Forest Service in the Manti La Sal National Forest in Utah. Two of these operations involve uranium exploration, while the third involves the installation of vent holes for the Pandora underground mine, whose entrance is located on BLM-managed land. Collectively, these operations have been authorized to disturb up to 7 acres of land. However, the Forest Service is currently reviewing a plan to authorize the Canyon Mine in the Kaibab National Forest in Arizona. This mine's plan of operations was initially approved in the mid-1980s and the

Forest Service is determining whether additional, more current environmental analysis must be undertaken to authorize this operation.

All 9 Mines on DOE's Lease Tracts Are on Standby

As part of is uranium leasing program, DOE oversees 31 lease tracts, which are in a variety of statuses.

- Eight tracts have a total of 9 uranium mines on them, all of which are on standby—that is, they are not actively extracting uranium.[34] These lease tracts cover about 6,900 acres, but the operations have disturbed only about 260 acres of land.
- Seven lease tracts have approved exploration plans, but no exploration work is ongoing.
- DOE has not approved any exploration or extraction plans for 14 lease tracts.
- The remaining 2 lease tracts have not been leased out.

According to DOE officials, no extraction activity has taken place on its lease tracts since 2006 for two reasons.[35] First, DOE officials reported that there has been limited incentive to explore or extract uranium on their lease tracts because there are no uranium processing mills in Colorado near the lease tracts.[36] Second, in October 2011, a federal district court ordered that no additional surface disturbance could take place on any DOE lease tracts until DOE completes an appropriate environmental analysis pursuant to NEPA.[37] DOE officials told us that a programmatic environmental impact statement is due to be released for public comment in late 2012.

AGENCY DATA INDICATE THAT FINANCIAL ASSURANCES ADEQUATELY COVER NEARLY ALL OPERATIONS, BUT BLM AND NRC DO NOT COORDINATE IN ESTABLISHING SOME ASSURANCES

As of January 2012, BLM, the Forest Service, and DOE reported $249.1 million in financial assurances, and these assurances appear to be generally adequate to cover the estimated reclamation costs for uranium operations on federal land, according to our analysis of agency data.[38] Agency data indicate that nearly all of these assurances ($247.6 million of the $249.1 million) are for operations that are at least partially on BLM-managed land.[39] Although almost all of these financial assurances were adequate to cover the estimated cost of reclamation, we identified some issues in how BLM oversees these assurances. We also found the value of financial assurances for two ISR operations had increased significantly, but that BLM and NRC did not coordinate their efforts to establish and review financial assurances for these operations. The remaining $1.5 million in financial assurances is for authorized operations on land managed by the Forest Service and for DOE lease tracts. According to our analysis of agency data, these financial assurances are adequate to cover the current estimated cost of reclamation for the operations that the two agencies oversee.

BLM Had Financial Assurances to Cover Reclamation Costs for Nearly All Operations, but Some Issues Exist Regarding Agency Oversight

As of January 2012, BLM had financial assurances of about $245.5 million for 144 authorized uranium operations, according to our review of BLM's Bond Review Report, and the financial assurances were adequate for all but 2 of the operations. Specifically, we found 1 operation where BLM field staff reported that the assurance in place was likely inadequate to reclaim an acid pit lake that had formed at an older, inactive open pit uranium mine in Wyoming. The operation has in place a financial assurance in the amount of $126,000, but the operator is in the process of developing a new reclamation estimate for BLM to review. In addition, we found 1 operation for which the financial assurance for a plan of operations in Utah was $16,000 less than the estimated reclamation costs.[40] In general, we found that most of the financial assurances for operations on BLM land are for less than $100,000.

During our review of BLM's data, we identified two issues related to BLM's Bond Review Report for overseeing financial assurance of uranium operations. First, we found inaccuracies in the information included in the report. Specifically, the Bond Review Report indicated that reviews of the financial assurances for 5 notice-level operations had not taken place in over 36 months, which is a year past the frequency that BLM guidance requires. According to BLM officials, these 5 operations had been reviewed within the correct time frames, but staff had entered an incorrect action code into

LR2000. We also found other instances during the course of our review where BLM staff had entered incorrect action codes into this system. LR2000 accepts hundreds of action codes, yet the agency does not have comprehensive guidance on all the action codes that can be used in LR2000.

Second, the Bond Review Report does not include financial assurances that are in place for expired operations. According to our review of agency data, there are 58 expired uranium operations on BLM land. One reason BLM officials offered for why the Bond Review Report does not include information on expired operations was because the financial assurances for these operations are smaller. However, the information we reviewed shows that 43 expired uranium operations had about $2 million in financial assurances and that some of these expired operations had assurances that were well above $100,000. In addition, we found the remaining 15 expired operations did not have any financial assurances in place. According to BLM officials, because these 15 operations were established prior to BLM's 2001 regulations that required financial assurances for all mining operations, it is reasonable that these operations do not have financial assurances. Nonetheless, these 15 operations do need to be reclaimed and, according to BLM staff, these operations may not be receiving the required oversight, which is evidenced by the fact that several of these operations were last inspected about a decade ago. The fact that these 15 operations have not been reclaimed or inspected in almost a decade suggests that oversight of expired operations could be improved.

BLM and NRC Do Not Coordinate when Establishing and Reviewing Assurances for ISR Operations

We found that two ISR operations—the Smith Ranch and Highland operations in Wyoming—account for $213 million in financial assurances, or 86 percent of the total financial assurances held for uranium operations on land managed by BLM. According to BLM officials, a portion of the financial assurances for these two operations also covers activities on land that is not managed by BLM, such as state or private land.[41] The required financial assurances for ISR operations on the Smith Ranch and Highland operations have increased from June 2011 through December 2011—from about $80 million to about $120 million for the Smith Ranch, and from about $80 million to about $93 million for Highland, although the size and disturbance of the operations at these two sites has not significantly changed. According to BLM,

NRC, and Wyoming state officials, this increase is due to a variety of factors, including new estimates of the additional work necessary to restore the groundwater at these sites. For example, the estimated number of cycles during which this groundwater is extracted and treated before being reinjected—known as a pore volume—has been increased from six to nine. The cost to restore groundwater at these sites has also increased because the operator had previously removed equipment necessary to restore the groundwater so the equipment could be used in other operating wellfields, and this equipment must now be either returned to these sites or replaced with other groundwater restoration equipment, according to NRC officials. In March 2008, the state of Wyoming issued a notice of violation to the operator for Smith Ranch and Highland that stated that the operator was not adhering to the schedule for restoring groundwater and that its estimate of the number of pore volumes and resources needed to restore the groundwater were too low. As a result, the state concluded that the total financial assurances in place at the time for the Smith Ranch and Highland operations—$38.4 million—should be increased immediately to $80 million to protect the public and that a more realistic estimate of the cost to reclaim the sites would be close to a total of $150 million.[42] According to Wyoming state officials we spoke with, this notice of violation was part of the process of requiring greater financial assurances for the Smith Ranch and Highland operations that has resulted in these operations now having a combined $212.7 million in financial assurances.

In examining the efforts to increase financial assurances for these two sites, we found that BLM and NRC did not coordinate their efforts with each other. According to Wyoming state officials, BLM field office staff generally provide comments and concurrence on the proposed financial assurances that operators submit annually. In contrast, NRC generally conducts its own independent review of the financial assurances it believes should be in place. In 2009, NRC and BLM enacted a memorandum of understanding intended to improve interagency cooperation in environmental assessments; facilitate the sharing of special expertise and information; and coordinate the preparation of studies, reports, and documents. However, this memorandum does not cover interagency coordination of the review of financial assurances.

Even though the financial assurances for the Smith Ranch and the Highland operations have increased significantly, the lack of federal coordination when establishing these financial assurances raises concerns about the adequacy of these financial assurances and the financial assurances associated with any future ISR operations that may be authorized. (For more information on active and pending ISR operations, see app. II.) According to our review, it appears that both BLM and NRC have expertise in different areas of the work needed to reclaim an ISR operation, and better coordination among these agencies would help ensure that all necessary factors have been considered. Specifically, BLM primarily has expertise in estimating the cost of reclaiming surface disturbances at a mining site, and NRC primarily has expertise in estimating the cost of restoring groundwater contaminated by radioactive material. NRC officials reported that some of this expertise was developed through overseeing reclamation activities at uranium processing mills where groundwater must be restored, buildings demolished, and monitoring wells plugged. However, NRC officials acknowledged that the scale of disturbance at an ISR site is much greater than at a mill, because of the thousands of wells that must be plugged and the surrounding surface reclaimed. In addition, restoring the underground water at these mining sites is a complex process because it must be restored to the background concentration, a maximum concentration that incorporates standards set by EPA, or alternate concentration limits as approved by NRC.[43] According to Wyoming state officials we spoke with, enhanced coordination between the federal agencies and also with the state could help to leverage each agency's particular expertise in reviewing financial assurances for ISR sites. These state officials told us that this coordination is even more important because ISR operators have had little experience with restoring groundwater at ISR wellfields to date in Wyoming. Specifically, at the Smith Ranch and Highland ISR sites, the state and NRC have approved groundwater restoration efforts at only 1 of the 19 wellfields according to Wyoming state and NRC officials.

The Forest Service and DOE Have Adequate Financial Assurances to Cover Reclamation Costs for Uranium Activity

The Forest Service and DOE have financial assurances for uranium operations that are adequate to cover the current estimated cost of reclamation for the sites they oversee, according to our analysis of agency data. Specifically, the Forest Service reported having about $42,000 in financial assurances for the three operations on its land, one of which consists of installing vent holes for a mine on adjacent BLM land, and the other two were for operations currently conducting exploration. The Forest Service handbook requires that all active financial assurances be reviewed annually, and our review found that all had been reviewed within appropriate time frames.

DOE reported about $1.5 million in financial assurances for its 29 tracts that have been leased out, with about $1.2 million of this total for a single lease tract with an inactive open pit uranium mine. Our review of DOE data indicates that these assurances were adequate as of the last time they had been reviewed—from 1996 through 2005 for 9 lease tracts and in 2008 or later for the remaining 22 tracts.[44] DOE officials told us they had not reviewed some of these financial assurances more recently because there has been little new activity on the lease tracts in recent years. DOE officials told us that they generally review financial assurances when a lessee makes a change to an exploration or mining plan on a lease tract.

FEDERAL AGENCIES DO NOT HAVE RELIABLE DATA ON THE NUMBER AND LOCATION OF ABANDONED URANIUM MINES OR THEIR ASSOCIATED CLEANUP COSTS

Federal agencies do not have reliable data on the number and location of abandoned uranium mine sites on federal lands and the potential cleanup costs associated with these sites, according to our review of agencies' databases and discussions with agency staff. We found that agency databases generally lack complete data and a common definition of an abandoned mine site, and contain information that has not been verified through field inspections. In addition, federal agencies do not have estimates of the potential total cleanup cost for abandoned uranium mine sites on the land they manage. According to agency officials, the cost to clean up these sites varies according to site-specific conditions, including the amount and type of work required at each site, and the total number of sites needing cleanup.

Federal Data on Abandoned Uranium Mines Are Unreliable

There are likely thousands of abandoned uranium mine sites on federal land where either exploration or extraction may have taken place, but the available federal data on these sites are generally unreliable. In particular, we found the following limitations with these data.[45]

Agencies' databases are incomplete. Three agency databases only partially track the commodity extracted, and one of them omitted sites with incorrect geographic coordinates. For example, according to BLM's database, there are an estimated 1,189 abandoned uranium mine sites on BLM-managed land. However, these data are based primarily on information from three states (Colorado, Utah, and Wyoming) because the BLM state offices in these states require their local field offices to enter the commodity that had been previously extracted from these abandoned mines.[46] Similarly, in the National Park Service's abandoned mine database, the commodity field is optional for agency staff to enter.[47] On the other hand, EPA's database, which estimates that there are 8,124 abandoned uranium mine sites on federal land, does not include some sites because they do not have specific geographic coordinates, according to agency officials. In addition, some of the databases have not been updated in years and do not track the extent to which extraction took place at each site, which would help indicate the type of cleanup work that might be required. For example, the Forest Service database lists an estimated 1,097 abandoned uranium mine sites; however, the status of many of these sites has not been updated since they were first entered in the database in the 1980s. In addition, the Forest Service and EPA databases do not track which abandoned mine sites have already been cleaned up. As a result, it is not possible to determine from the agency data how many sites remain to be cleaned up.

Agencies do not have a consistent definition of an abandoned mine site. We found agencies do not share a consistent definition of an abandoned mine site, and even within an agency the definition may not be consistently applied by various field offices or staff. These inconsistencies pose a problem when trying to combine multiple databases or to compare data across multiple agencies. For example, because of a lack of a consistent site definition, EPA officials told us that the agency faced a challenge in trying to combine data from multiple sources in order to provide more complete information on abandoned uranium mine sites.[48] In addition, even within a single agency, staff may use different definitions of an abandoned mine site when entering data into a database. For example, a BLM official told us that field staff may enter each abandoned mine feature, such as a waste rock pile or a mine opening, as a separate site, instead of grouping these features into one entry. According to a 2007 EPA report on its efforts to develop a database on abandoned uranium mine sites, the lack of a consistent definition leads to problems with determining how many sites exist, since even a single agency's database may contain mines meeting a variety of definitions.[49] In March 2008, we highlighted the lack of a consistent definition for abandoned hardrock mine sites and the way in which this inconsistency contributes to a wide variation in estimates of the number of abandoned mines.[50] At that time, we developed a consistent definition of an abandoned hardrock mine site, and used it to develop a more robust estimate of abandoned mines by applying it across multiple databases. According to EPA officials we interviewed, federal agencies involved with abandoned mines have used a regular interagency forum, called the Federal Mining Dialogue, to discuss the issue of a lack of a common definition of a mine site but have not yet reached agreement on how to address this issue.[51]

Agency databases contain sites that have not been verified through field inspections. According to agency officials, field inspection is the best way to determine an abandoned mine's location and features, such as posing physical safety and environmental hazards, to discover new abandoned mine sites, and to figure out what cleanup may be required at an abandoned mine site. However, field inspections also require more resources because agency staff must try to cover large areas of land, sometimes in risky or inaccessible conditions, such as mountainous or rocky areas. Currently, the National Park Service and BLM are in the process of verifying the condition of abandoned mine sites on their land. According to National Park Service officials, the agency received $3.3 million over 3 years to verify how many abandoned mine sites, including uranium mines, it has on the land it manages, and to verify cleanup needs at these sites, a process the agency hopes to complete by September 30, 2012. On the basis of preliminary results from this field inspection, National Park Service officials told us that of the 46 abandoned uranium mine sites on their land, 25 remain to be cleaned up. Since 2009, some inventory efforts of abandoned mines on BLM land have been under way in Arizona, New Mexico, and Wyoming, but not all BLM offices in these states require their staff to track the commodity that was extracted at abandoned mine sites.[52] Table 5 and appendix III provide more specific information on the limitations of each agency's database on abandoned uranium mines. BLM, EPA, and Forest Service officials told us that their agencies do not have an accurate number of abandoned mine sites and their location because no laws or regulations require the agencies to track abandoned mines and that the agencies do not have sufficient resources to collect this information. Specifically, officials from BLM and EPA explained that any tracking of sites is done voluntarily to help with their mission. In addition, BLM and Forest Service officials told us that they have not had sufficient funds to conduct field inspection verification on all their known abandoned mine sites on the lands they manage and that to do so would be costly, requiring additional financial and staff resources. At current funding levels, according to a May 2011 draft feasibility study, it will take BLM 13 years and $39 million to finish inspecting all known abandoned mine sites on its land, including the ongoing inventory work in Arizona, New Mexico, and Wyoming.[53]

Table 5. Limitations with Four Federal Agencies' Databases on Abandoned Uranium Mines

Agency	Database name[a]	Limitations with these databases				
		Partially tracks the commodity extracted	Does not track the extent to Which extraction took place at a site	Does not track which sites have been cleaned up	Used an inconsistent definition of a site	Some sites in the database have not been verified through field inspection
BLM	Abandoned Mine/Site Cleanup Module	X	X		X	X
The Forest Service	Forest Service Abandoned Mineral Lands Database	X	X	X	X	X
National Park Service	Servicewide Abandoned Mineral Lands Database	X				
EPA	Technologically Enhanced Naturally Occurring Radioactive Materials Uranium Location Database		X	X	X	X

Source: GAO analysis of information from BLM, the Forest Service, the National Park Service, and EPA

[a] The BLM, Forest Service, and National Park Service databases refer to abandoned uranium mine sites on the land they manage. The EPA database refers to sites on all federal land.

Cleanup Costs for Abandoned Uranium Mines Vary Greatly, Depending on Site-Specific Conditions

In addition to not knowing how many abandoned uranium mines are on federal land, BLM, the Forest Service, EPA, and the National Park Service do not have information on the total cost of cleaning up abandoned uranium mines. Officials noted that cleanup costs are determined not only by the total number of mines that need cleanup, but also by site-specific conditions, including the amount and type of work required at each site. Agency officials explained that each abandoned mine site has distinctive characteristics and requires a unique cleanup plan based on, among other things, its size, accessibility, the need for heavy equipment, and the level of contamination.

Agency officials we spoke with generally agreed that cleanup costs at individual sites could range from several thousand dollars to hundreds of millions of dollars. These officials also agreed that most of the work is likely to fall within one of the following three cleanup categories: addressing safety hazards, conducting surface reclamation, and conducting environmental remediation.[54] However, officials cautioned that sometimes cleanup at a site requires work across two or all of these categories. Figure 3 illustrates some of the activities that can take place in these cleanup categories.

Table 6. Ranges of Costs for Conducting Cleanup Activities at Selected Abandoned Uranium Mine Sites

Primary cleanup work conducted at a site	Number of abandoned uranium sites examined	Range of cost (in 2011 dollars)
Address physical safety	6	$1,800–$33,000
Conduct surface reclamation	6	$2,500–$98,000
Conduct environmental remediation	6	$203,000–$193,000,000[a]

Source: GAO analysis of information received from DOE, the Forest Service, and the National Park Service.

[a] Four of the six examples provided by agencies for this category are based on estimates and not on actual cleanup costs.

The agencies also provided us with examples of costs that have been incurred at 18 abandoned uranium mine sites. Table 6 provides a range of costs associated with cleanup efforts depending on the type of work conducted at each site. It is important to note that these cost ranges are not exhaustive and that some cleanup costs for other abandoned uranium mine sites could fall outside these cost ranges.

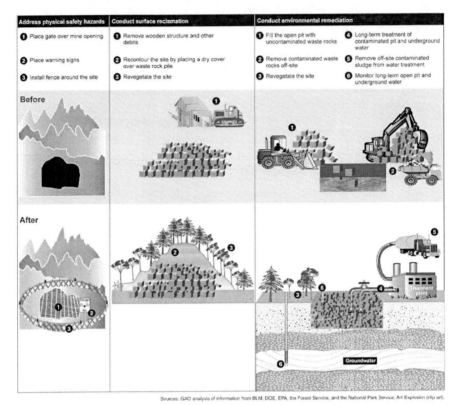

Note: This figure is illustrative and does not include all possible activities that may take place based on site-specific conditions.

Figure 3. Examples of Cleanup Activities That Could Take Place at Abandoned Uranium Mine Sites.

Some examples of the factors that can contribute to the variability in the costs for cleanup at abandoned uranium mine sites include the following.

- *Number of safety hazards that need to be addressed:* BLM and National Park Service officials told us that most of the work they have conducted to date on abandoned uranium mines is designed to mitigate safety hazards. Costs for this type of work have ranged from $1,800 to close 2 mine openings in Arches National Park in Utah to $33,000 to backfill 11 mine openings with waste rock at the Canyonlands National Park in Utah.[55] A BLM official cautioned that future costs to address sites with physical safety hazards can be higher

because BLM has generally addressed safety hazards that are the least costly to clean up because of limited available funding.[56]
- *Extent to which surface reclamation needs to be conducted:* The primary purpose of activities under this category is to return the land to as near its previous appearance as possible through recontouring and revegetating disturbed land. According to DOE documents, the costs to reclaim the surface ranged from about $2,500 for closing 2 mine openings, recontouring 70 cubic yards of dirt, and revegetating 1 acre of disturbed land at the Nine Mile Hill Mines on BLM-managed land in Colorado to nearly $98,000 for more extensive reclamation work at the Hawk Mine Complex on lands managed by BLM in Colorado.[57] The work at this site primarily focused on the installation of multiple gates over mine openings, backfilling 500 cubic yards of surface pits with waste materials, recontouring 6,800 cubic yards of waste rock materials from 8 waste rock piles, and revegetating 4 acres of disturbed area.
- *Extent to which environmental remediation must be undertaken:* Most of the activities in this category are designed to mitigate significant environmental hazards. Officials from BLM, the Forest Service, National Park Service, DOE, and EPA told us that few abandoned uranium mine sites have undergone remediation, but cited two instances in which this work has occurred or is ongoing and proved to be costly and the costs varied significantly.[58] For example, according to our review of agency documents, the Pryor Mountain Mine, located on land managed by the Forest Service in Montana, cost about $200,000 to clean up, and involved environmental remediation to remove contaminated soil and waste rock that posed a human health risk. The site, located close to an Indian reservation and near hiking trails and campsites, initially presented levels of radioactive contamination that were up to 369 times higher than normal background levels. At another site—the 320-acre open pit Midnite Mine site in Washington state—costs are estimated to be as high at $193 million by the time remediation is complete, according to EPA documents.[59] Most of this cost is for treating acid rock drainage in two large open pits that contain millions of gallons of water and then filling these pits with 33 million tons of waste materials. Some mine sites that require environmental remediation also require long-term—defined as longer than 5 years—maintenance and monitoring, especially if contaminated water requires treatment. For example, one

of the largest costs (approximately $32 million) associated with environmental remediation at the Midnite Mine site is for monitoring and treating surface and underground water. EPA estimates that this water will need to be treated in perpetuity.

Additional information on these and other abandoned uranium mine sites is presented in appendix IV.

CONCLUSION

Having adequate financial assurances to pay for reclamation costs for federal land disturbed by uranium operations is critical to ensuring that the land is returned to its original state if operators fail to complete the reclamation as required.

BLM, the Forest Service, DOE, and NRC play key roles in establishing and reviewing these financial assurances for uranium operations on federal land.

We found that nearly all of the uranium operations on federal land had adequate financial assurances, according to our analysis of agency data. However, we found some limitations in agencies' oversight of uranium operations' financial assurances, which raise some concerns about these financial assurances. In particular, ISR operations account for a large proportion of financial assurances in place for uranium operations on federal land and have recently been increasing for some operations, yet there is little coordination between BLM and NRC when establishing and reviewing these assurances.

This lack of coordination raises concerns about the adequacy of the financial assurances in place for existing ISR operations and for those ISR operations that are awaiting approval.

Both BLM and NRC have specific expertise in assessing certain aspects of the reclamation activities that are required at ISR sites, but have no process in place to share this information and leverage their expertise. Without such coordination, the agencies cannot be confident that the assurances they establish for ISR operations will be adequate to cover the costs of reclamation.

BLM relies on its LR2000 database and Bond Review Report to provide information that supports its oversight of financial assurances. However, data entered into LR2000 are sometimes inaccurate and not always updated in a timely manner in keeping with BLM's requirements.

Moreover, the Bond Review Report does not examine expired operations, yet we found that some of these operations have large financial assurances in place or have not been inspected in 10 years.

Without complete, timely, and accurate information in LR2000 and the Bond Review Report, the usefulness of these management tools to BLM may be diminished and may limit effective oversight of uranium operations.

Finally, identifying the number, location, and cost of cleanup of abandoned mines is a challenging task for federal agencies. However, this process has been made more difficult because the agencies have not been able to reach agreement on a consistent definition for what constitutes an abandoned mine site.

Without a consistent definition, data collection efforts are hampered and agency databases cannot be combined to provide a more complete picture of abandoned mines on federal land.

RECOMMENDATIONS FOR EXECUTIVE ACTION

To help better ensure that financial assurances are adequate for uranium mining operations on federal land, we are recommending the following three actions.

- The Secretary of the Interior and the Chairman of the Nuclear Regulatory Commission should enhance their coordination on financial assurances for ISR operations through the development of a memorandum of understanding that defines roles and promotes information sharing.
- The Secretary of the Interior should direct the Director of the Bureau of Land Management to take the following actions to improve oversight of financial assurances:
  - include information on expired mine operations in the annual Bond Review Report process, and
  - develop guidance to ensure accurate and prompt data entry in LR2000.

To enhance data collection efforts on abandoned mines, we recommend that the Secretaries of the Interior and of Agriculture and the Administrator of the Environmental Protection Agency work to develop a consistent definition of abandoned mine sites for use in data-gathering efforts.

Agency Comments

We provided a draft of this report to the Department of Agriculture, the Department of Energy, the Department of the Interior, the Environmental Protection Agency, and the Nuclear Regulatory Commission for review and comment.

All of these agencies concurred with our recommendations. In particular, NRC recognized that development of a memorandum of understanding on financial assurance reviews could be beneficial to NRC and BLM, and plans to pursue such an agreement with BLM.

NRC noted that development of a memorandum of understanding that adequately addresses both agencies' regulatory oversight may be challenging and stated that the agency may pursue other, less formal methods of coordination with BLM if a memorandum of understanding cannot be developed.

In addition, DOE stated that a national database for uranium mining activities would be useful, and the agency agreed there is a need for federal agencies with uranium mines on their land to have common definitions and to use these definitions when gathering information that could be used to determine reclamation needs.

Similarly, EPA agreed that a consistent definition of abandoned mine sites would be useful, and will work with other relevant agencies to develop a definition, if possible. Furthermore, EPA commented that our report lacked specificity with regard to our use of the terms "reclamation" and "remediation."

We have modified our report to include more specific definitions of each of these terms and clarified what each of these terms means in the context of the report. EPA and the Department of the Interior also provided us with technical comments, which we have incorporated as appropriate.

Sincerely yours,

Anu K. Mittal
Director,
Natural Resources and Environment

APPENDIX I. OBJECTIVES, SCOPE, AND METHODOLOGY

Our objectives were to (1) compare Bureau of Land Management (BLM), Forest Service, and Department of Energy (DOE) oversight of uranium exploration and extraction operations on federal land; (2) determine the number and status of uranium operations on federal land; (3) examine the coverage and amounts of financial assurances in place for reclaiming current uranium operations on federal land; and (4) examine what is known about the number and location of abandoned uranium mines on federal land and their potential cleanup costs.

To compare BLM, Forest Service, and DOE oversight of uranium exploration and extraction on federal land, we reviewed federal laws, regulations, and guidance, as well as prior GAO reports and other studies on hardrock mining operations.[60]

We also spoke with BLM, Forest Service, and DOE officials in headquarters and field offices, and BLM state offices in Arizona, Colorado, New Mexico, Utah, and Wyoming—five states with large uranium deposits. We also reviewed DOE lease contracts. To understand the interagency relationship among BLM, the Forest Service, and DOE, as well as the these agencies' relationship with the states, we reviewed memorandums of understanding among these parties.

We also spoke with state representatives of mining and environmental agencies in Arizona, Colorado, New Mexico, Texas, Utah, and Wyoming to discuss how they coordinate with federal agencies while reviewing uranium operations and their financial assurances.

We discussed relevant issues for hardrock operations and financial assurances with representatives from the mining industry, state geological services, and an environmental group. We also examined relevant regulations from EPA and NRC and spoke with officials from these agencies.

To determine the number and status of uranium operations on federal land, we gathered information from BLM, the Forest Service, and DOE. To identify uranium operations on BLM land, we requested that BLM provide an extract from its LR2000 database for operations—both notices and plans of operations—that were in an authorized, expired, or pending status and listed "uranium" or "uranium and other minerals" as the commodity that was being targeted.

To determine the reliability of these data, we spoke with a BLM information technology official responsible for administering the system; BLM state and field office staff who enter information into the system; and

BLM managers at the agency's Washington, D.C., headquarters office who use information from the system. We also reviewed database documentation, and we determined the LR2000 data were sufficiently reliable for our purposes.

We used these data to administer a web-based survey to BLM field staff responsible for overseeing uranium operations in 25 field offices across eight states—Arizona, Colorado, Nevada, New Mexico, Oregon, South Dakota, Utah, and Wyoming. We asked these staff to provide the status of these operations based on the most recent information available using the following eight status levels and definitions, which we developed in consultation with BLM staff:

- exploration permitting (e.g., operator is in the process of obtaining permits to conduct exploration at the site),
- exploration (e.g., operator is preparing the site for exploration or conducting exploration work at the site; concurrent reclamation may also be taking place),
- extraction permitting (e.g., operator is in the process of obtaining permits to extract uranium at the site),[61]
- extraction (e.g., operator is preparing the site for extraction or actively extracting uranium at the site; concurrent reclamation may also be taking place),
- standby (e.g. operator is authorized to explore or extract, but is not doing so),
- reclamation (e.g., reclamation is taking place at the site following the end of exploration or extraction activities),
- closed (e.g., reclamation is complete and financial assurance has been released), and
- other.

As part of this survey, we asked BLM staff to provide copies of the documentation they consulted when determining the status of the operation, such as inspection reports or correspondence with operators, and we used these documents to verify the reported status.

For field offices overseeing a large number of operations, we requested they provide documents for 10 operations they oversaw, which we selected randomly. We also asked BLM staff if there had been any uranium extracted at the operation in the last 5 years. Prior to sending out this survey, we pretested it with officials from 3 BLM field offices and revised some of the survey questions based on their input. We received responses to our survey from all 25 field offices, and we sent follow-up questions based on their survey responses to clarify certain responses or to ask for additional information. Because the Forest Service and DOE oversee fewer uranium operations than BLM, we did not use our survey to collect information on the status of these operations; instead, we gathered this information through interviews with agency officials and agency documents.

The Forest Service compiled information on its uranium operations by contacting Forest Service officials who were located in National Forests where uranium operations are located. The Forest Service also provided documentation on these operations that we used to verify the information it provided. DOE provided information on its lease tracts that it maintains as part of its program.

We used DOE's annual status report on its lease tracts to help to verify the reported status levels along with conversations with DOE officials. For both the Forest Service and DOE, we used interviews with officials along with relevant documentation to determine the reliability of these data, and we determined they were sufficiently reliable for our purposes.

To examine the financial assurances in place for uranium mining on BLM land, we reviewed information in BLM's Bond Review Report, which aggregates data on financial assurances from BLM's LR2000 database, including the required amount of the financial assurance for an operation, the amount of the financial assurance in place, and when it was last reviewed. As part of this analysis, we examined whether the financial assurances in place were adequate to cover the estimated costs of reclamation; we did not determine whether the estimated costs for reclamation were sound because that was outside the scope of our review.

Since the Bond Review Report relies on LR2000 data, we used our data reliability assessment of LR2000 detailed above to help determine whether the data in the report were reliable.

In addition, we obtained a copy of the specifications that were used to create the Bond Review Report and examined the report to identify outliers in the data or incomplete fields and used BLM documents or discussions with BLM staff to clarify any issues we identified. We determined that BLM's financial assurance data in its Bond Review Report were sufficiently reliable for the purposes of our review.

Because BLM's Bond Review Report contains only information on authorized operations, we gathered information on financial assurances from LR2000 for the expired operations. To examine the financial assurances in place for uranium operations on Forest Service land and DOE's lease tracts, we examined data provided by these agencies. Specifically, we compared the financial assurance amounts that were required with the amounts that were in place.

As we did for our analysis of BLM's data, we examined whether the financial assurances in place were adequate to cover the estimated costs of reclamation; we did not determine whether the estimated costs for reclamation were sound because that was outside the scope of our review. To determine the reliability of the data from the Forest Service and DOE, we interviewed agency staff who gathered these data, and we used supporting documentation to corroborate the information that was reported.

We determined that these data were sufficiently reliable for our purposes. To learn about the number and location of abandoned uranium mines on federal land, we reviewed data from BLM, the Forest Service, EPA, the National Park Service, and DOE, which are all involved in efforts to track and clean up abandoned uranium mines.

We received and analyzed data from databases these agencies maintain on abandoned uranium mines. We also reviewed pertinent documents that accompanied some of these databases and other agency documentation, such as studies or reports that describe the status of abandoned uranium mines on lands managed or leased by these agencies. We conducted two sets of semistructured interviews with officials in charge of abandoned mine programs at all of these agencies—before and after we reviewed the data and documentation—to gather more information about these databases, including identifying limitations and determining the reliability of the data in the databases. We also conducted interviews with officials from the U.S. Geological Survey, which maintains the data used by the Forest Service. We also interviewed staff from BLM field offices and state agencies in the states where most uranium deposits are located to get more information on the number and location of abandoned uranium mines and to hear their perspectives on the federal databases. As a result of our efforts, we determined that these data were not sufficiently reliable to establish a definite number of abandoned uranium mines. However, because these were the only federal data available, we have used them in the report only to discuss in general terms the number of potential abandoned uranium mine sites that may exist on federal lands, and we have described the limitations associated with these data. To describe the potential cleanup costs posed by abandoned uranium mines, we reviewed relevant literature and conducted semistructured interviews with officials from the federal agencies in charge of abandoned mines.[62] On the basis of this information, we identified three distinct cleanup categories that we and agency officials believe are most representative of the types of actions that take place at abandoned uranium mine sites. In developing these categories, we consulted with officials from all five agencies in charge of cleaning up abandoned uranium mine sites, and they agreed with our approach and our categories. These categories are not mutually exclusive, and cleanup work at a site could fall within multiple categories, especially at larger or more contaminated sites. These cleanup categories included actions taken to

- address safety hazards, which means that most cleanup activities at the site are intended to mitigate safety hazards;
- conduct surface reclamation, which means that most cleanup activities at the site are intended to return the land to its appearance before mining activities took place; and
- conduct environmental remediation, which means that most cleanup activities at the site are intended to deal with removing land and water contamination that poses a threat to the environment and human health. These activities can also include long-term—defined as longer than 5 years—maintenance and monitoring.

We also asked officials from these five agencies to provide us with examples that are illustrative of the range of costs associated with performing such cleanup work. We asked for examples of sites that have already been cleaned up and have definitive costs, or information on sites that have detailed cost estimates. We received 18 examples from the agencies, which are divided equally across the three cleanup categories. Fourteen examples are for past work and contain actual cleanup costs; 4 examples, all in the environmental remediation category, are for work that is still to be completed and are based on estimated costs. For better comparison purposes, we reported these cost numbers in 2011 dollars. For each example, we asked for and received documentation that describes in detail the work performed at each site. For the sites that have not been cleaned up yet, we received pertinent documentation, such as records of decision or consent decrees. To get a better understanding of uranium mining in general, we conducted site visits to Colorado and Wyoming to examine uranium operations. We visited these states because they have a variety of uranium operations involving several federal agencies. In Colorado, we spoke with BLM, DOE, and state officials involved in overseeing uranium operations.

We also spoke with representatives of a uranium company and toured some uranium operations including some underground mines that were on standby on land managed by BLM and a few abandoned mine sites. In addition, we toured two DOE lease tracts and examined reclamation work that had been performed on these tracts. In Wyoming, we met with BLM and state officials involved in overseeing uranium operations and spoke with representatives of some uranium companies. In addition, we toured an in situ recovery operation and examined the various components of this operation. We conducted this performance audit from June 2011 through May 2012 in accordance with generally accepted government auditing standards. Those standards require that we plan and perform the audit to obtain sufficient, appropriate evidence to provide a reasonable basis for our findings and conclusions based on our audit objectives. We believe that the evidence obtained provides a reasonable basis for our findings and conclusions based on our audit objectives.

APPENDIX II. INFORMATION ON IN SITU RECOVERY OPERATIONS ON BLM LAND THAT ARE EXTRACTING URANIUM, ON STANDBY, OR AWAITING FEDERAL AUTHORIZATION

This appendix provides information on in situ recovery (ISR) operations on land managed by BLM. Some of these operations are not entirely on federal land, but rather include state and private land. The Forest Service and Department of Energy officials reported that they do not have any ISR operations on land they manage.

Table 7. Information on ISR Operations Located on BLM-Managed Land and Their Associated Financial Assurance

Name	Location	Operator	Financial assurance amount (dollars in millions)	Status
Highland	Wyoming	Cameco	$92.73	Extracting uranium.
Smith Ranch	Wyoming	Cameco	120.04	Extracting uranium.
Willow Creek	Wyoming	Uranium One	16.3	Extracting uranium.
Gas Hills	Wyoming	Cameco	3.47	Waiting for BLM authorization. Authorized by the

Appendix II. (continued)

Name	Location	Operator	Financial assurance amount (dollars in millions)	Status
				Nuclear Regulatory Commission (NRC).
Hank and Nichols	Wyoming	Uranerz	6.8	Waiting for BLM authorization. Authorized by NRC.
Lost Creek	Wyoming	UR Energy	2.09	Waiting for BLM authorization. Authorized by NRC.
Reynolds Ranch	Wyoming	Cameco	Smith Ranch financial assurance covers this operation.	Authorized by BLM and NRC but not extracting uranium.
Ross	Wyoming	Strata	No decision on financial assurance yet.	Waiting for BLM and NRC authorization.
Ruth	Wyoming	Cameco	$0.18	BLM has not yet received a plan of operations for this operation. Authorized by NRC.
Dewey Burdock	South Dakota	Powertech	No decision on financial assurance yet.	Waiting for BLM and NRC authorization.

Source: GAO analysis of BLM and NRC information.

APPENDIX III. DETAILED INFORMATION ON FEDERAL ABANDONED MINE DATABASES

This appendix provides information on federal databases that contain information on abandoned uranium mines, and the limitations that we identified for each database.

Table 8. Information on Federal Abandoned Mine Databases and Their Limitations

Agency	Database name	Number of abandoned uranium mines listed in the database[a]	Mines cleaned up to date listed in the database[a]	Number of abandoned uranium mines in the database that remain to be cleaned up[a]	Limitations with the data
BLM	Abandoned Mine-Site Cleanup Module (AMSCM)[b]	3,038	1,849	1,189	• Entering the mined commodity in this database is optional. Only three BLM state offices (Colorado, Utah, and Wyoming) require BLM staff to enter information on the mined commodity. • The database does not provide information on the extent to which extraction took place at a site. • BLM officials from various field offices who enter information in the database use their own definition of a "site." • Some sites have not been verified through field inspection.
The Forest Service	Forest Service Abandoned Mineral Lands Database, which relies entirely on the U.S. Geological Survey's (USGS) Mineral Resources Data System (MRDS)[c]	1,097	Unknown	Unknown	• MRDS has not been updated since 1995. Also, it does not include information on the major commodity mined for over 22,000 of its records. • The database does not provide updated information on the extent to which extraction took place at a site. • The definition used by the Forest Service for a site is different than the definition used by the USGS for its MRDS database.

Agency	Database name	Number of abandoned uranium mines listed in the database[a]	Mines cleaned up to date listed in the database[a]	Number of abandoned uranium mines in the database that remain to be cleaned up[a]	Limitations with the data
National Park Service	Servicewide Abandoned Mineral Lands Database	46	21	25	• Few sites have been verified through field inspection. • MRDS does not identify whether a site has already been cleaned up or not. • MRDS database contains many duplicates. • Entering the commodity field is optional for National Park Service staff.

Source: GAO analysis of information from BLM, the Forest Service, National Park Service, and EPA.

[a] The BLM, Forest Service, and National Park Service databases refer to abandoned uranium mine sites on the lands they manage. The EPA database refers to sites on all federal land.

[b] According to a BLM official, AMSCM is a stand-alone internal database housed at the National Operations Center in Denver, Colorado, which is separate from BLM's larger LR2000 data system.

[c] According to a Forest Service official, the Forest Service is in the process of starting work on its own database on abandoned mines. The new database will also keep track of which sites have been cleaned up to date.

APPENDIX IV. EXAMPLES OF CLEANUP ACTIVITIES AT ABANDONED URANIUM MINE SITES

This appendix provides information on cleanup activities at 18 abandoned uranium mine sites. Fourteen sites have been cleaned up and have actual cleanup costs, while 4 examples provided by agencies are based on estimates and not on actual cleanup costs.

Table 9. Examples of Cleanup Activities at Abandoned Uranium Mine Sites

Mine name, location / (federal agency managing the land)	Description of the mine	Summary of cleanup work performed or planned at the site[a]			Total cost (in 2011 dollars)
		Address physical safety hazards	Conduct surface reclamation	Conduct environmental remediation	
Mines where cleanup focused on physical safety					
Salt Valley Wash Mines, Utah (National Park Service)	Two small underground mines, each with one shaft (vertical mine opening) in Arches National Park, dating from the 1940s.	Backfilled two shafts by hand with 24 and 63 cubic yards of adjacent waste material	None	None	$1,818
Loma Mines, Colorado (Bureau of Land Management)	Conventional underground mines located beneath a bluff 2 miles from an interstate highway.	Backfilled two mine adits (horizontal mine opening) with trash and wood debris, and closed them with polyurethane foam	None	None	2,105
Terry Mine, Utah (National Park Service)	Conventional underground mine located in the Capitol Reef National Park, within one-quarter mile of a main road.	Backfilled a shaft with 85 cubic yards and an adit with 50 cubic yards of waste materials Erected two fences of 800 and 960 feet in length to exclude grazing cattle Placed warning signs around the site	Revegetated the site Burned wooden structures	None	10,443

Mine name, location / (federal agency managing the land)	Description of the mine	Summary of cleanup work performed or planned at the site[a]			Total cost (in 2011 dollars)
		Address physical safety hazards	Conduct surface reclamation	Conduct environmental remediation	
Whirlwind, Utah (National Park Service)	Conventional underground mine located about 400 feet above the elevation of a lake in Glen Canyon National Recreation Area. The cleanup crew and equipment were flown in by helicopter.	Demolished structures Backfilled adits with steel, wood, and other debris Closed a drill hole with polyurethane foam Posted four warning signs	Demolished an 800-square-foot steel ore bin	None	11,448
White Rim, Utah (National Park Service)	Four conventional underground mines located in Glen Canyon National Recreation Area. One site is located about 1 mile from the park's Visitors Center and another about 1 mile from a campground.	Installed steel gates over five adits Backfilled by hand one adit using 8 cubic yards of material	None	None	22,499
Lathrop Canyon 1-8, Utah (National Park Service)	Conventional underground mine located in Canyonlands National Park that was developed in the late 1950s. The crew accessed the site by foot and the equipment was flown in by helicopter.	Closed 11 adits using various methods Installed warning signs throughout the site	None	None	33,021
Mines where cleanup focused on surface reclamation					
Nine Mile Hill Mines, Colorado (Bureau of Land Management)	Conventional underground mines located above a public highway.	Backfilled two small adits with waste rock material using an excavator	Recontoured 70 cubic yards of waste rock materials Revegetated 1 acre of land	None	2,524

Table 9. (Continued)

Mine name, location / (federal agency managing the land)	Description of the mine	Summary of cleanup work performed or planned at the site[a]			Total cost (in 2011 dollars)
		Address physical safety hazards	Conduct surface reclamation	Conduct environmental remediation	
Mesa No. 5, Colorado (Bureau of Land Management)	Conventional underground mine that contained a waste rock pile, which affected an adjacent, intermittent stream.	Closed two small-diameter ventilation shafts with polyurethane foam Backfilled a mine opening with 5,200 cubic yards of waste rock materials and trash and debris	Recontoured 10,200 cubic yards of waste rock material Covered the recontoured area with topsoil excavated from a nearby site Revegetated 4 acres of land	None	12,963
Northern Light Mines, Colorado (Bureau of Land Management)	Conventional underground mine.	Placed wood debris from demolished structures in mine openings Installed gates over 3 adits Backfilled 5 additional shafts with waste rock	Recontoured 600 cubic yards of waste rock Covered the recontoured area with topsoil Revegetated 2 acres of land	None	17,121
Rainy Day, Utah (National Park Service)	Conventional underground mine located in the Capital Reef National Park 4 miles from the main road. The site was accessible by foot.	Placed debris from demolished structures in mine adits Backfilled 12 adits with earth from the disturbed slope using a backhoe	Demolished structures Corrected areas of severe erosion and built drainage controls	None	30,768
New Verde Mine, Colorado (Bureau of Land Management)	Single underground large mine. This is a historic site where parts of the operation were left in place and preserved.	None	Demolished and disposed of structures offsite Removed trash and	None	78,524

Mine name, location / (federal agency managing the land)	Description of the mine	Summary of cleanup work performed or planned at the site			Total cost (in 2011 dollars)
		Address physical safety hazards	Conduct surface reclamation	Conduct environmental remediation	
Hawk Mine Complex, Colorado (Bureau of Land Management)	A complex of underground mines that started operations in 1948, consisting of eight separate and distinct mine sites, six mine access ramps, three adits, and one surface pit.	Placed debris from eight locations in mine openings Backfilled seven mine openings with waste rock Installed gates at three mine openings Closed nine small ventilation shafts and 132 exploration drill holes using polyurethane foam	Backfilled 500 cubic yards of surface pits with waste rock materials Recontoured 6,800 cubic yards of waste rock materials from eight waste rock piles Covered the recontoured area with 1,000 cubic yards of topsoil Revegetated 4 acres of land Recontoured 22,000 cubic yards of waste rock materials Covered the recontoured area with topsoil Revegetated 6 acres of land debris offsite	None	97,589
Mines where cleanup focused on environmental remediation					
Pryor Mountain Mine, Carbon County,	Two separate mines developed in the 1950s wheel-drive roads, and large equipment was brought in by helicopter	Installed gates over three adits Backfilled a number of exploration pits	Revegetated all of the disturbed areas within the site	Removed human health risks related to the site (no details were available of the	203,238

Table 9. (Continued)

Mine name, location / (federal agency managing the land)	Description of the mine	Summary of cleanup work performed or planned at the site[a]			Total cost (in 2011 dollars)
		Address physical safety hazards	Conduct surface reclamation	Conduct environmental remediation	
Montana (the Forest Service)	located in an area where hiking and camping take place. The site is also used as a sacred ground by a nearby Indian tribe. The site was accessible by four-.	Removed 4- to 8- foot highwalls (edge of the mine) Removed one collapsed structure		actual work conducted)	
Workman Creek Uranium Mines, Gila County, Arizona (the Forest Service)	The site, developed in the 1950s, encompasses eight mines on steep hillsides located near campgrounds. Waste rock piles contain elevated levels of carcinogenic and radioactive elements, and there is concern of these materials getting into major water supplies that serve the Phoenix metropolitan area.	Plan to: Install warning signs	Plan to: Backfill the excavated areas with clean soil Recontour some areas to establish stability and prevent water runoff Cut off road access to the site	Plan to: Backfill all 33 mine openings with 30,500 cubic yards of waste rock, some of which is contaminated, and close them with polyurethane foam Remove 500 cubic yards of contaminated waste rock piles from the campgrounds and creek side and place in a repository on site	600,000b (estimate)
San Mateo Uranium Mine, New Mexico (the Forest Service)	The site, which operated between 1957 and 1971, is located in a remote location with limited public access. The waste rock pile is toxic and radioactively contaminated, and storm water runoff from this pile flows into a nearby creek.	Plan to: Install an 8-foot-high chain-link fence to enclose approximately 17 acres necessary to exclude wildlife and livestock from destroying the vegetation	Plan to: Recontour and revegetate approximately 35 acres to further reduce windblown transport of any	Plan to: Consolidate and cover 180,000 cubic yards of contaminated waste rock pile Conduct ongoing maintenance to repair	3,095,750b (estimate)

Mine name, location / (federal agency managing the land)	Description of the mine	Summary of cleanup work performed or planned at the site[a]			Total cost (in 2011 dollars)
		Address physical safety hazards	Conduct surface reclamation	Conduct environmental remediation	
White King Lucky Lass, Oregon (the Forest Service)	This site consists of two conventional open pit mines for a combined 140 acres of disturbed land. It operated between 1955 and 1965. The site had three large waste rock piles of approximately 1.26 million cubic yards and two large pits that cover approximately 5 and 14 acres, which are full with millions of gallons of water. Carcinogenic and radioactive contaminants were found at the site and a creek runs next to the mine and received discharge from this contaminated pit. This site was added to EPA's National Priority List in 1995.	Installed three-strand barbed wire fencing around wetlands and reclaimed waste stockpiles	Regraded, replaced topsoil, capped with a dry cover system, and revegetated the waste rock piles Restored and revegetated other disturbed areas	Removed contaminated soil from the stockpiles Relocated the flow of the creek into historic channels and constructed three wetland areas to prevent runoff into the creek Installed 10 wells for groundwater monitoring Plan to perform long-term monitoring and regular neutralization of the pit water to prevent any acidic water from reaching the creek	5,939,087
Riley Pass Mine, Harding County, South Dakota (the Forest Service)	This site, which operated in the 1950s and 1960s, involves 12 mine groups and spreads over approximately 1,000 acres. The site consists of numerous open pits, waste rock piles, and five	None	Plan to: Reshape the highwalls Fill or reshape the erosion gullies	residual contamination erosion of the cap material and of the drainage channels after heavy rainfall events Plan to: Establish a series of sediment control measures, such as sediment ponds, to control runoff	74,733,520b (estimate)

Table 9. (Continued)

Summary of cleanup work performed or planned at the site[a]

Mine name, location / (federal agency managing the land)	Description of the mine	Address physical safety hazards	Conduct surface reclamation	Conduct environmental remediation	Total cost (in 2011 dollars)
	sediment ponds. The area is prone to erosion, and the site poses safety concerns from unstable highwalls. The site also poses health and environmental risks from heavy metals and radiation. Two mines have already been cleaned up and cleanup at a third is ongoing. The U.S. government is currently involved in a bankruptcy proceeding with potentially responsible parties to recover costs for the remaining cleanup.		Stabilize the fragile soils and revegetate the area	Excavate and place contaminated material in designed repositories, or cap the contaminated material in place The Forest Service estimates that a long-term maintenance effort will be needed for at least 100 years because of the fragile soil and climate conditions	
Midnite Mine, Stevens County, Washington (Bureau of Land Management)	This is a more than 320-acre open pit mine that operated from 1954 to 1981. Approximately 33 million tons of waste material was dug up from six large pits, two of which have not been backfilled and are full of water. Numerous piles of waste materials are also located throughout the site. High levels of toxic and radioactive chemicals are at the site. Acidic water drains into a nearby creek.	Plan to: Build a fence around the site and boulder barriers around the contaminated waste piles	Plan to: Cover the four pits that were backfilled with a thick dry cover, clean soil, and vegetation Grade and cover waste piles and areas cleaned of waste throughout the site with fresh soil and vegetation Conduct long-term	Plan to: Empty out the two pits full with acid water and treat this water at a water treatment plant on site Cover the bottom of these pits with a thick drainage layer where water can collect and install a water removal system along with filling the pits	193,000,000[b] (estimate)

Mine name, location / (federal agency managing the land)	Description of the mine	Summary of cleanup work performed or planned at the site[a]			Total cost (in 2011 dollars)
		Address physical safety hazards	Conduct surface reclamation	Conduct environmental remediation	
	Some cleanup work at the site has already been conducted. This site was added to EPA's National Priority List in 2000.		maintenance and monitoring of the dry cover systems and the vegetation to mitigate acid rock drainage	with waste rock and covering the pits with a thick vegetated cover Build a new water treatment plant to treat millions of gallons of acidic groundwater and dispose of sludge Build sediment barriers to prevent sediment migration from the mine drainages into the creek Conduct ongoing maintenance and monitoring of water treatment and remove sludge for at least 140 years	

Sources: GAO analysis based on information provided by DOE, the Forest Service, and the National Park Service.

[a] It is important to note that we summarized some of the key activities performed at the site; other activities may also have taken place at the site.
[b] This amount is an estimate, since cleanup has not yet been completed or has not started at the site.

End Notes

[1] GAO, *Hardrock Mining: Information on Abandoned Mines and Value and Coverage of Financial Assurances on BLM Land,* GAO-08-574T (Washington, D.C.: Mar. 12, 2008).

[2] Under the Federal Land Policy Management Act of 1976, the Bureau of Land Management (BLM) issued regulations, effective in 1981, that required all mining operators to reclaim BLM land disturbed by hardrock mining. In 2001, BLM regulations began requiring all mining operators to provide financial assurances before beginning exploration or mining operations on BLM land. The Forest Service began requiring reclamation and financial assurances in 1974.

[3] See 43 C.F.R. § 3809.420 (2011); 36 C.F.R. § 228.8 (2011).

[4] These financial assurances, also referred to as bonds, include a variety of financial instruments. For example, a surety bond is a third-party guarantee that an operator purchases from a private insurance company approved by the Department of the Treasury. The operator must pay a premium to the surety company to maintain the bond. These premiums can vary depending on various factors, including the amount of the bond and the assets and financial resources of the operator, among other factors.

[5] GAO, *Hardrock Mining: BLM Needs to Revise Its Systems for Assessing the Adequacy of Financial Assurances,* GAO-12-189R (Washington, D.C.: Dec. 12, 2011); *Abandoned Mines: Information on the Number of Hardrock Mines, Cost of Cleanup, and Value of Financial Assurances,* GAO-11-834T (Washington, D.C.: July 14, 2011); *Hardrock Mining: BLM Needs to Better Manage Financial Assurances to Guarantee Coverage of Reclamation Costs,* GAO-05-377 (Washington, D.C.: June 20, 2005).

[6] Remediation refers to the containment or treatment of hazardous substances. Remediation work at a mine site can involve removing contaminated waste rock or soil to an off-site location. In addition, contaminated surface or underground water may need to be remediated using a water treatment facility. As described above, reclamation activities may include measures to isolate, remove, or control toxic materials, work that could also be characterized as remediation. Environmental remediation could also be required after a mine is abandoned if reclamation was not properly completed or if new or unforeseen problems arise after abandonment.

[7] We did not include tribal lands in our review of uranium operations on federal land. Currently, there are no active uranium mining operations on tribal lands; however, there are abandoned uranium mines on these lands that will require extensive remediation in some cases. We have included an example of the anticipated remediation actions needed at one such site later in our report. In addition, EPA, DOE, NRC, the Bureau of Indian Affairs, and the Indian Health Service are implementing a 5-year plan to address the health and environmental impacts of uranium contamination in the Navajo nation.

[8] For the purposes of describing the work conducted on abandoned uranium mines, we are using the term "cleanup" to encompass the variety of activities necessary to address conditions at abandoned mine sites.

[9] Under U.S. mining laws, minerals are classified as locatable, leasable, or saleable. The General Mining Act of 1872 17 Stat. 91 (codified at 30 U.S.C. § 22 et. seq.) allows individuals to stake claims for locatable minerals, such as uranium, copper, lead, zinc, magnesium, gold, and silver. For the purposes of this report, we use the term "hardrock minerals" as a synonym for "locatable minerals." The Mineral Leasing Act of 1920, 41 Stat. 437 (codified at 30 U.S.C. § 181) created a leasing system for certain minerals such as coal, gas, oil and other fuels, and chemical minerals, which are known as leasable minerals. In 1955, the Multiple Use Mining Act of 1955, 69 Stat. 367 (codified at 30 U.S.C. § 601) removed common varieties of sand, stone, and gravel from development under the Mining Act, and these minerals are known as saleable minerals.

[10] Production data are for pounds of uranium oxide (U_3O_8) extracted from federal, state, and private land.

[11] At the mill, the mined uranium ore is crushed, ground, and then fed to a leaching system that uses resin and chemicals to separate uranium from the ore. The resulting yellow slurry—called yellowcake—is washed, dried, and stored in steel drums. Yellowcake subsequently undergoes a number of processing steps (conversion, enrichment, and fuel fabrication) to become fuel for nuclear power plants.

[12] According to EIA, the amount of uranium that can be produced economically at a market price of $50 a pound using ISR—known as a mineral's reserves—is greater than the amount that can be produced through underground and open pit uranium mining. EIA, *U.S. Uranium Reserve Estimates* (Washington, D.C.: July 2010). Current market prices are close to $50 a pound. At a higher market price of $100 a pound for uranium, the reserves for uranium that can be recovered using underground and open pit uranium mining exceed the reserves for ISR, according to this EIA report.

[13] Susan Hall, USGS, *Groundwater Restoration at Uranium In-Situ Recovery Mines, South Texas Coastal Plain* (Reston, Virginia: 2009).

[14] DOE's regulations are codified in 10 C.F.R. § 760.1 (2012).

[15] In the area covered by DOE's leasing program, mined ore contains both uranium and vanadium. This ore is delivered to the processing facility as a combined commodity, and the separate uranium and vanadium minerals are recovered during processing.

[16] On February 27, 2012, the same court ruled that certain reclamation activity, including actions to address dangers to public health and safety and the environment, could continue. *Colorado Environmental Coalition et al. v. Office of Legacy Management et al.* 2012 U.S. Dist. LEXIS 24126 (D. Colo. Feb. 27, 2012).

[17] Arizona, Colorado, Utah, and Wyoming have been approved to implement this permit program, known as the National Pollutant Discharge Elimination System program, at the state level. Texas has approval for a partial program.

[18] New Mexico, Texas, Utah, and Wyoming, four states with uranium deposits, have been approved to implement the UIC program at the state level. Colorado implements its UIC program jointly with EPA.

[19] EPA is currently reviewing its existing groundwater standards under 40 C.F.R. pt. 192.

[20] Colorado, New Mexico, Texas, Utah, and Wyoming require financial assurances for the full cost of reclamation, while Arizona does not require financial assurances for the full cost of reclamation.

[21] BLM's regulations for hardrock mining are in 43 C.F.R. subpt. 3809.

[22] Forest Service regulations governing the surface use of National Forest System land in connection with hardrock mining are in 36 C.F.R. Part 228, subpt. A.

[23] DOE's previous environmental assessment was conducted on the uranium leasing program in 1995.

[24] BLM may review the reclamation cost estimate more frequently if there is cause to believe the reclamation cost estimate is insufficient. A financial assurance for an operation may need to be reviewed annually when it covers an operation that will grow over time according to the timeline submitted in the plan of operations, a practice known as phased bonding.

[25] BLM does not have an agreement covering joint bonding with Arizona.

[26] Forest Service guidance directs its staff to obtain financial assurances to cover the estimated reclamation costs for mining operations on National Forest System lands.

[27] Unlike BLM and Forest Service, many states provide for the collection of royalty payments. For example, Arizona, Colorado, New Mexico, Utah, and Wyoming charge a royalty for uranium extraction. In the current Congress, the proposed Uranium Resources Stewardship Act (HR1452, 112th Cong. (2011)) would require a royalty charge of at least 12.5 percent on uranium extracted from federal land and rental charges for the land being mined. The money collected would then be used to clean up abandoned uranium mines and mill sites.

[28] The royalty paid differs by lease tract. Leases for tracts held before 2008 require payment of a bid royalty and a base royalty. The bid royalty is a competitive bid made by operators to acquire the lease. The base royalty is set by DOE based on ore production on the lease. Leases rebid on in 2008 require payment of a bid royalty only. The bid royalty is considered the "production royalty" for these lease tracts.

[29] This count does not necessarily represent individual mine sites because multiple plans of operations may cover a single mine, among other reasons. In addition, the data in this section reflect site status as of January 2012, and the number of uranium operations can fluctuate over time.

[30] This information on acreage reflects the total amount of the authorized area that can be disturbed. However, actual disturbance can often be much smaller, according to BLM officials.

[31] Staff were allowed to select multiple statuses for an operation on our survey. As a result, the sum of responses will exceed the number of operations.

[32] On our survey, we used the terms "mine permitting" and "production." For the purposes of using consistent terms in this report, we are substituting the terms "extraction permitting" and "extraction."

[33] GAO, *Standards for Internal Control in the Federal Government*, GAO/AIMD-00-21.3.1 (Washington, D.C.: November 1999).

[34] One of these lease tracts has 2 mines on it. Of the 9 total mines, 1 is an open pit mine and the other 8 are underground mines.

[35] DOE officials also reported that no exploration activity has taken place on the lease tracts since 2010.

[36] The capacity to process uranium in mills is currently limited, with only one operating uranium mill in the United States, in Blanding, Utah. In Colorado, a uranium mill known as the Piñon Ridge mill is currently in the process of obtaining the necessary permits before it can begin construction.

[37] In February 2012, the court modified the injunction to allow certain surface-disturbing activities, including those that are absolutely necessary to conduct the environmental analysis.

[38] The data in this section reflect the financial assurances in place as of January 2012, and the value of financial assurances for uranium operations can fluctuate over time.

[39] For operations that involve a combination of BLM and state or private land, BLM's Bond Review Report generally reports the financial assurance for the entire operation, not just the portion on BLM-managed land, and that is what we are reporting. However, BLM does not report information on financial assurances for the portions of mining operations in Arizona that are not on BLM-managed land because the agency does not have a joint bonding agreement with Arizona.

[40] According to BLM officials, the agency has contacted the new owner of this operation about the need to increase the financial assurance amount.

[41] According to BLM officials, the financial assurances held for uranium operations are not broken out by the entity that manages the surface.

[42] Wyoming Department of Environmental Quality, "In Situ Uranium Permits 603 and 633, Notice of Violation, Docket No. 4231-08" (Cheyenne, Wyoming, 2008).

[43] Alternate concentration limits can be set if groundwater cannot be restored to background levels, and these limits are based on site-specific conditions at a location. See 10 C.F.R. pt. 40 app. A (2012).

[44] According to DOE, the financial assurances for the 2 lease tracts that were not leased out were last reviewed in June 2008.

[45] DOE also maintains information on abandoned uranium mine sites in a centralized database that also tracks other information related to its uranium leasing program. However, we did not include this database in this analysis, since, according to DOE officials, DOE cleaned up all of its 190 abandoned uranium mine sites from 1996 to 2011 on its lease tracts.

[46] According to a BLM official, the board in charge of managing the BLM database on abandoned mines has recently decided to eliminate the commodity field from the database.

[47] New hardrock mining claims may not be located on land managed by the National Park Service, and none of the legacy claims currently in the system are for uranium. Therefore, it is highly unlikely that there will be any active uranium operations on National Park Service land. The agency is, however, involved in overseeing efforts to clean up abandoned uranium mines on its land.

[48] In 2006, EPA combined data from 19 different databases into one single database. This database primarily includes data from state agencies and BLM's state offices in Arizona, Colorado, New Mexico, Utah, and Wyoming; data from the USGS; as well as some databases with limited number of records from a few states outside these areas, such as California, Montana, South Dakota, and Texas.

[49] EPA, *Technical Report on Technologically Enhanced Naturally Occurring Radioactive Materials from Uranium Mining,* Volume 2 (Washington, D.C.: August 2007).

[50] GAO, *Hardrock Mining: Information on Abandoned Mines and Value and Coverage of Financial Assurances on BLM Land,* GAO-08-574T (Washington, D.C.: Mar. 12, 2008). In this report, we defined an abandoned hardrock mine site as all associated facilities, structures, improvements, and disturbances at a distinct location associated with activities to support a past operation of minerals locatable under the general mining laws.

[51] The Federal Mining Dialogue, established in 1995, is a forum for discussing and coordinating abandoned mine-related issues among federal agencies. EPA serves as the lead agency. Regular participating agencies include BLM, EPA, the Forest Service, National Park Service, and USGS. Other agencies, such as the Department of Justice or the U.S. Army Corps of Engineers, participate when issues of interest arise.

[52] According to BLM officials, BLM was directed to stop any inventory efforts from 1999 to 2009 to focus on cleaning up the already identified abandoned mines because of funding limitations.

[53] BLM, *Draft Feasibility Study for AML Inventory Validation and Physical Safety Closures* (Washington, D.C.: May 2011).

[54] As discussed earlier, reclamation activities, broadly speaking, may also include environmental remediation. In this section, we distinguish between "surface reclamation," which includes activities such as recontouring and revegetating the land, and "environmental remediation," which involves the containment and treatment of hazardous substances or other toxic materials.

[55] The cleanup costs provided in this section are in 2011 dollars.

[56] According to a BLM draft feasibility study, if current funding levels are maintained in the future, it will cost BLM $362.7 million to clean up all of the known abandoned mines, including uranium mines, with physical safety hazards, requiring 77 years.

[57] BLM contracted with DOE to conduct this reclamation work on its land.

[58] Both of these examples are from EPA's Superfund program.

[59] This site is located partially on BLM-managed land and tribal lands within the Spokane Indian Reservation. The federal government reached a settlement agreement with mining companies responsible for the site, under which these companies agree to conduct cleanup work and reimburse certain response costs of the federal government. The government agreed to contribute approximately 20 percent of the expected cleanup costs.

[60] We did not include tribal lands in our review of uranium operations on federal land. Currently, there are no active uranium mining operations on tribal lands; however, there are abandoned uranium mines on these lands that will require extensive remediation in some cases. We have included an example of the anticipated remediation actions needed at one such site in our report. In addition, the Environmental Protection Agency (EPA), DOE, the Nuclear Regulatory Commission (NRC), the Bureau of Indian Affairs, and the Indian Health Service are implementing a 5-year plan to address the health and environmental impacts of uranium contamination in the Navajo nation.

[61] On our survey, we used the terms "mine permitting" and "production." For the purposes of using consistent terms in this report, we are substituting the terms "extraction permitting" and "extraction."

[62] For the purposes of describing the work conducted on abandoned uranium mines, we are using the term "cleanup" to encompass a variety of activities necessary to address these abandoned mine sites.

In: Uranium Mining and Management
Editors: J. Dunn and D. Arnold
ISBN: 978-1-62257-412-4
© 2012 Nova Science Publishers, Inc.

Chapter 2

EXCESS URANIUM INVENTORIES: CLARIFYING DOE'S DISPOSITION OPTIONS COULD HELP AVOID FURTHER LEGAL VIOLATIONS[*]

United States Government Accountability Office

WHY GAO DID THIS STUDY

Uranium is a key component in the production of nuclear energy and nuclear weapons. The Department of Energy (DOE) manages the nation's surplus uranium, which is derived in part from former nuclear weapons production. In 2008, DOE published a uranium management plan that set a target for DOE uranium sales and transfers to avert harm to the domestic uranium industry. In 2009, DOE began using natural uranium to pay for cleanup work at a former uranium enrichment facility in Ohio, without having identified such transactions in its 2008 plan.

As directed, GAO reviewed DOE's uranium management program. This report examines (1) DOE's uranium transactions and plans for future transactions, (2) the extent to which these transactions were consistent with DOE's uranium management plan, and (3) the extent to which these

---
[*] This is an edited, reformatted and augmented version of the Highlights of GAO-11-846, a report to congressional committees, dated September 2011.

transactions were consistent with federal law. GAO reviewed transaction documents and contracts and interviewed knowledgeable DOE, contractor, and uranium industry officials and uranium market analysts.

WHAT GAO RECOMMENDS

GAO recommends that DOE update its uranium management plan and suggests that Congress consider authorizing DOE to, among other things, retain the proceeds of future uranium transactions. DOE agreed to update its uranium management plan but disagreed that its actions did not comply with federal fiscal law. GAO maintains, however, that DOE's comments do not undermine the conclusion that the department violated the miscellaneous receipts statute.

WHAT GAO FOUND

In a series of seven transactions from December 2009 through June 2011, DOE used 1,873 metric tons of natural uranium to pay for $256 million in cleanup services provided by two contractors at the Portsmouth, Ohio, enrichment facility, and additional transactions are planned. Six out of seven of these transactions involved the United States Enrichment Corporation (USEC), former operator of the Portsmouth facility. DOE released 1,473 metric tons of uranium, and USEC provided $194 million in cleanup services at the Portsmouth facility. Among other activities, USEC's services included removing chemical and hazardous materials from the plant. The seventh transaction involved a second contractor. In June 2011, DOE released 400 metric tons of uranium, and the contractor agreed to provide $62 million in decontamination and decommissioning services. DOE officials said the department expects to continue transferring natural uranium to this contractor for cleanup services through 2013.

DOE's uranium transactions have been consistent with parts of its uranium management plan but not with others. The plan states that DOE would adhere to a target for uranium sales and transfers of no more than 10 percent of annual domestic fuel requirements for uranium. DOE's releases of uranium into the commercial market did not exceed the annual target specified in the plan, ranging from 5 percent of demand in 2008 to 6 percent in 2010—

well below the 2008 plan's designated target. With regard to other provisions, however, DOE has departed somewhat from the plan. For example, the department has deviated from the schedule of uranium transfers articulated by the plan, allowing more uranium to enter the market sooner than cited.

DOE's uranium transactions with USEC were sales authorized by the USEC Privatization Act, but they did not comply with federal fiscal law. The USEC Privatization Act requires that before a uranium sale, DOE must determine that the materials are surplus to national security needs; that the department is receiving fair market value; and that the sales will not adversely affect the domestic uranium mining, conversion, and enrichment industries. GAO found that DOE met these requirements. Nevertheless, by not depositing the value of the net proceeds from the sales of uranium into the Treasury, DOE violated the miscellaneous receipts statute. This statute requires an official or agent of the government receiving money from any source on the government's behalf to deposit the money in the Treasury. As GAO found when it reviewed a similar series of transactions in 2006, DOE provided the uranium to USEC for sale to a third party and allowed USEC to keep the proceeds of the sales. Even with no money changing hands, GAO concludes that an amount equivalent to the value that went to USEC should have gone to the Treasury. By not depositing an amount equal to the value of the uranium into the Treasury, DOE has inappropriately circumvented the power of the purse granted to Congress under the Constitution.

ABBREVIATIONS

DOE   Department of Energy
NNSA   National Nuclear Security Administration
USEC   United States Enrichment Corporation

September 26, 2011

The Honorable Dianne Feinstein
Chairman
The Honorable Lamar Alexander
Ranking Member
Subcommittee on Energy and Water Development
Committee on Appropriations

United States Senate

The Honorable Rodney P. Frelinghuysen
Chairman
The Honorable Peter J. Visclosky
Ranking Member
Subcommittee on Energy and Water Development
Committee on Appropriations
House of Representatives

Uranium—a naturally occurring radioactive element—is used in nuclear weapons as well as in fuel for nuclear power plants. In the United States, 20 percent of the nation's electricity comes from nuclear power, and growing energy demand and concerns about carbon dioxide emitted when fossil fuels are burned have sparked interest in increasing the use of nuclear power. A healthy and reliable domestic uranium industry is considered essential to ensuring that nuclear power remains a viable option for supplying the nation's energy needs.

From the 1940s, the Department of Energy (DOE) and its predecessor agencies have processed uranium as a source of nuclear material for defense and commercial purposes. A key step in this process is the enrichment of natural uranium, which raises its concentration of uranium- 235, the form, or isotope, that undergoes fission to release enormous amounts of energy in nuclear reactors and weapons. The enrichment process results in two principal products: (1) enriched uranium hexafluoride, which can be further processed for specific uses, such as nuclear weapons or fuel for power plants, and (2) leftover "tails" of uranium hexafluoride, which are also called depleted uranium because the material is depleted in uranium-235 compared with natural uranium. Since 1993, uranium enrichment activities at DOE-owned uranium enrichment plants have been performed by the United States Enrichment Corporation (USEC), a former government-owned corporation that was privatized in 1998.

DOE maintains inventories of natural, enriched, and depleted uranium in excess of its needs. This inventory comes from a variety of sources, including the dismantling of some of the nation's nuclear weapons or leftover material from before 1993. The department stores most of its uranium at its Portsmouth Gaseous Diffusion Plant, a uranium enrichment facility in Piketon, Ohio, that ceased operations in 2001, and at its Paducah Gaseous Diffusion Plant, a similar facility currently operated by USEC in Paducah, Kentucky.

In March 2008, we reported on DOE's options for its inventory of depleted uranium.[1] We recommended that the department develop a comprehensive uranium management assessment containing detailed information on the types and quantities of depleted, natural, and enriched uranium managed by DOE and a comprehensive assessment of the department's options for this material. In December 2008, with input from the uranium industry, DOE published its "Excess Uranium Inventory Management Plan" detailing the amount of uranium held by the department and what plans it had at that time for selling or transferring uranium to the commercial market. The purpose of DOE's plan was to provide the general public and interested stakeholders more specific information and enhanced transparency with respect to DOE's preliminary plans for its excess uranium transactions.[2] The plan detailed the amount and type of uranium in the department's possession and DOE's disposition strategy at the time. Among other details in the plan, DOE committed to generally restricting its annual uranium sales and transfers to 10 percent of domestic nuclear fuel requirements but also noted that it may exceed 10 percent in any given year for certain special purposes. Shortly thereafter, in July 2009, DOE announced its intent to use some of its natural uranium to compensate USEC—in lieu of cash payment—for accelerated environmental cleanup work the company was conducting at the Portsmouth facility. This work was intended to prepare the facility for decontamination and decommissioning. In August 2010, DOE entered into a new contract with the firm Fluor-B&W Portsmouth to decontaminate and decommission the Portsmouth facility.[3] Subsequently, DOE announced a second round of uranium transactions—this time with the new contractor instead of USEC—to similarly compensate it for some of its services at Portsmouth.

The conference report accompanying the fiscal year 2010 Energy and Water Development and Related Agencies Appropriations Act directed us to review DOE's overall uranium management plan, including the department's oversight and implementation strategy, and to assess certain uranium transactions for consistency with federal law.[4] Accordingly, this report examines (1) DOE's transactions using its excess uranium and its plans for such transactions in the future, (2) the extent to which these transactions have been consistent with DOE's excess uranium management plan, and (3) the extent to which these transactions are consistent with federal law.

To examine DOE's uranium transactions for cleanup services, we reviewed, among other things, DOE documents detailing the transactions the department has engaged in involving its uranium, assessments of the value of uranium in each transaction, and analyses of the impact of DOE's activities on the uranium market. To examine the extent to which DOE's activities have been consistent with its excess uranium management plan, we analyzed the plan and compared the uranium activities the plan projected against DOE's actual uranium transactions. To determine the extent to which DOE's uranium transactions are consistent with federal law, we reviewed statutes governing DOE's uranium activities, including the USEC Privatization Act, as well as relevant fiscal laws, such as the miscellaneous receipts statute.[5] For all of our objectives, we interviewed officials at DOE's headquarters in Washington, D.C., and at the Portsmouth/Paducah Project Office in Lexington, Kentucky. We interviewed uranium industry representatives at selected mining, milling, conversion, enrichment, and fabrication firms about DOE's uranium management plan, the commercial uranium market, and the impact of DOE's activities on the uranium industry. We selected firms in the uranium industry to obtain information from each stage of the nuclear fuel cycle. We also interviewed nuclear industry trade representatives, market analysts, uranium brokers, and utilities. Appendix I describes our scope and methodology in more detail.

We conducted this performance audit from November 2010 through September 2011, in accordance with generally accepted government auditing standards. Those standards require that we plan and perform the audit to obtain sufficient, appropriate evidence to provide a reasonable basis for our findings and conclusions based on our audit objectives. We believe that the evidence obtained provides a reasonable basis for our findings and conclusions based on our audit objectives.

BACKGROUND

Before uranium can become nuclear fuel to produce energy or be used in weapons, it must be mined from the earth. Mining firms in the United States extract uranium by conventional means, such as open-pit and underground mining, as well as by means of a liquid that leaches uranium from the ground. The product from these techniques is a substance called yellowcake. Yellowcake on its own cannot fuel nuclear reactors and weapons. Rather, it is shipped to a conversion facility, where the yellowcake is converted to uranium hexafluoride (a gas when heated) for the enrichment process. Uranium comprises a mix of several isotopes, or forms of the same element with different atomic weights. Less than 1 percent of natural uranium found in yellowcake is the isotope uranium-235—the fissile isotope used in nuclear reactors and nuclear weapons. After conversion, enrichment firms use one of several processes to increase the amount of uranium-235 to concentrations suitable for generating nuclear power or for nuclear weapons. To be suitable as fuel for nuclear reactors, natural uranium must be enriched to a concentration of from 3 to 5 percent uranium-235. This fuel is referred to as low- enriched uranium. Natural uranium enriched to a concentration of over 90 percent uranium-235 is highly enriched uranium, which is considered weapons-grade material. For more detailed information about the nuclear fuel cycle, see appendix II.

Initially, the federal government was the only entity providing domestic enrichment services in the United States. More recently, however, domestic uranium enrichment activities have been performed by private industry. USEC is one of several firms that provide enrichment services to utilities operating nuclear power plants. It has provided enrichment services using DOE-owned facilities since 1993, when it began functioning as a government-owned corporation. In 1998, USEC began functioning as a private corporation, which today runs the Paducah Gaseous Diffusion Plant in Kentucky. USEC ran the Portsmouth Gaseous Diffusion Plant in Piketon, Ohio, until 2001, when DOE contracted the firm to maintain the plant in cold-standby status for a number of years until the department was ready to decontaminate and decommission it.[6] USEC is currently seeking funding to open a new enrichment facility, the American Centrifuge Plant, at the Portsmouth site.[7]

The market for uranium works somewhat differently from other commodity markets. In one of two ways, uranium buyers, such as utilities, purchase uranium and the services to convert it into nuclear fuel. First, buyers can obtain uranium under long-term contracts with sellers in the "term" market. Second, sellers can make their uranium available for immediate sale in a forum called the "spot" market. Transaction details about sales through both long-term contracts and the spot market are ordinarily considered business proprietary information. Uranium typically changes ownership through a process called a book transfer. Book transfers do not usually involve the physical movement of uranium, generally occurring at conversion and enrichment facilities, which tend to maintain large quantities of yellowcake or uranium hexafluoride on site for their customers. Uranium transactions are conducted directly between buyers and sellers, but brokers also match buyers with sellers for a fee. In addition, speculators may hold and sell uranium strategically to profit from swings in the price of the material.

DOE Has Used Excess Uranium to Pay for Cleanup Services, and Additional Transactions Are Planned

Since 2008, DOE has engaged in transactions involving excess uranium to pay two contractors for cleanup services at the Portsmouth Gaseous Diffusion Plant. Most of the uranium went to USEC to prepare the Portsmouth facility for decontamination and decommissioning. DOE plans additional transactions involving excess uranium.

DOE Has Used Nearly 1,900 Metric Tons of Excess Uranium to Pay for More Than $250 Million in Cleanup Services

From December 2009 through June 2011, DOE used 1,873 metric tons of its excess natural uranium to pay for $256 million in cleanup services at its Portsmouth facility (see table 1). During this period, the department completed seven transactions with two firms.

DOE's first six transactions took place with USEC. In these transactions, DOE released in total about 1,473 metric tons of uranium valued at about $194.3 million. In return, USEC provided accelerated cleanup services to prepare the Portsmouth facility for eventual decontamination and decommissioning. For example, USEC removed and disposed of chemical and hazardous materials, including electrical equipment containing polychlorinated biphenyls, toxic chemicals that the Environmental Protection Agency states have been demonstrated to cause cancer. Other work USEC performed included relocating a cooling water line and identifying excess equipment suitable for recycling.

One uranium transaction to date has also occurred between DOE and Fluor-B&W Portsmouth. This firm began activities to decontaminate and decommission the Portsmouth facility in March 2011, according to a DOE official. In June 2011, DOE released 400 metric tons of uranium valued at nearly $62 million to Fluor-B&W Portsmouth as payment for additional cleanup services at the Portsmouth facility.

Table 1. Net Value of Natural Uranium DOE Used to Pay for Cleanup, December 2009 through June 2011

Date	Recipient	Dollars per kilogram	Metric tons of uranium	Value
December 2009	USEC	$112.63	201.90	$22,740,662
March 2010	USEC	109.27	201.52	22,020,735
May 2010	USEC	111.55	226.32	25,246,385
July 2010	USEC	111.51	250.82	27,970,088
October 2010	USEC	132.89	242.74	32,256,667
March 2011	USEC	182.95	349.99	64,030,962
June 2011	Fluor-B&W Portsmouth	154.33	400.20	61,763,235
Total			**1,873.49**	**$256,028,734**

Source: GAO analysis of DOE data.

In these transactions, the value DOE received for each lot of natural uranium was reduced by the transaction costs both USEC and FluorB&W Portsmouth expected to incur to carry out the seven transactions (see table 2). These costs, which included charges for such things as storage cylinder handling and inspections, record keeping, and sales management, totaled almost $4 million. To account for these costs in the first six transactions, USEC reduced the value of the uranium transactions by 1 percent. Fluor-B&W Portsmouth reduced the value of its June 2011 transaction by substantially more—almost 2.8 percent—to account for sales costs. Fluor-B&W Portsmouth expects to discount all future transactions by a similar percentage as well, according to company representatives. In addition, under its contract with the department, Fluor-B&W Portsmouth also sought cost reimbursement from DOE for expenses associated with uranium handling and inspection and setting up what the parties referred to as a "uranium transfer management program." According to Fluor-B&W Portsmouth representatives, Fluor-B&W Portsmouth was not a participant in the uranium market before it entered into its contract with DOE, which required the company to establish processes and procedures to manage 10 anticipated transactions over two and a half years. DOE plans nine additional transactions of natural uranium with Fluor-B&W Portsmouth through 2013, according to agency documents.

Table 2. Uranium Sales and Other Transaction Costs

Date	Recipient	Sales costs	Other transaction costs	Total costs	Percentage of value
December 2009	USEC	$195,000	$230,000	$425,000	1.9
March 2010	USEC	195,000	155,000	350,000	1.6
May 2010	USEC	170,000	155,000	325,000	1.3
July 2010	USEC	135,000	195,000	330,000	1.2
October 2010	USEC	135,000	195,000	330,000	1.0
March 2011	USEC	262,348	0	262,348	0.4
Subtotal		$1,092,348	$930,000	$2,022,348	1.0
June 2011	Fluor-B&W Portsmouth	$1,748,822	$60,209	$1,809,031	2.8
Total		$2,841,170	$990,209	$3,831,379	1.5

Source: GAO analysis of DOE data.

DOE Plans Additional Transactions Involving Excess Uranium but Has No Plans to Transfer or Sell Depleted Uranium

In addition to the natural uranium that DOE anticipates it will release to Fluor-B&W Portsmouth for cleanup services through 2013, DOE also maintains other inventories of natural uranium. In 2008, DOE stored approximately 4,500 metric tons of uranium that does not currently meet commercial specifications for manufacturing nuclear fuel. According to DOE's December 2008 uranium management plan, this uranium would require considerable processing before it could meet commercial standards. The plan states that some of this material would eventually be processed and offered for use in the commercial market over a number of years. According to DOE, however, some of the material is so contaminated that it is no longer under consideration for processing, and DOE is uncertain what its ultimate disposition will be.

In addition to natural uranium, DOE maintains inventories of enriched and depleted uranium that are in excess of the department's needs. For example, at the end of fiscal year 2010, DOE had 89 metric tons of excess highly enriched uranium in its inventories. To dispose of highly enriched uranium, DOE's National Nuclear Security Administration (NNSA), a semiautonomous agency within DOE that is responsible for the management of the nation's nuclear weapons program, has reduced the enrichment level of some of this uranium so it is potentially usable as nuclear fuel in the Tennessee Valley Authority's nuclear power reactors. Some of the down-blended material has also gone to support DOE's American Assured Fuel Supply Program, which ensures, among other things, access to nuclear fuel for civilian reactors in foreign countries that have good nonproliferation credentials.

According to agency officials, DOE also has approximately 750,000 metric tons of depleted uranium tails that it stores in about 63,000 metal cylinders in storage yards at its Paducah and Portsmouth enrichment plants. A product of the enrichment process, this depleted uranium has historically been considered of limited use, but increases in uranium prices have potentially made it profitable to re-enrich some of the tails to further extract uranium-235. We reported in June 2011 that at May 2011 uranium prices and enrichment costs, DOE's tails have a net value of $4.2 billion.[8] This estimate is very sensitive, however, to changing uranium prices, which have been extremely volatile, as well as to the availability of sufficient enrichment capacity.

USEC has publicly announced an interest in re-enriching some of DOE's tails beginning in 2012. USEC plans to shut down operations at DOE's Paducah facility, depending on market conditions, and also plans to replace some of the Paducah facility's production capacity with the new centrifuge-based uranium enrichment plant it is constructing. USEC is considering continued operation of the Paducah facility beyond May 2012. According to USEC, processing depleted uranium could contribute toward maintaining operations at Paducah and retaining 1,200 employees the company might otherwise have to lay off. DOE officials, however, said that the department has no current plans to sell or re-enrich depleted uranium tails.

DOE'S TRANSACTIONS DID NOT EXCEED TARGETS SET BY ITS URANIUM MANAGEMENT PLAN, BUT DOE'S ACTIVITIES WERE NOT CONSISTENT WITH THE PLAN IN OTHER WAYS

DOE's excess uranium transactions have been consistent with parts of its uranium management plan but not with others. Specifically, the amount of uranium the department sold or transferred is less than the target of 10 percent of annual domestic fuel requirements that DOE established under the 2008 plan. With regard to other provisions, however, DOE has departed somewhat from the plan. For example, DOE has deviated from the schedule of uranium transfers articulated by the plan, resulting in more uranium entering the market much sooner than cited.

DOE's Uranium Transactions Have Not Exceeded the Target of 10 Percent of Domestic Uranium Demand Specified by the Plan

The total amount of uranium that DOE sold or transferred from January 2008 to June 2011 has stayed below the target specified in the department's December 2008 uranium management plan. The plan stated that DOE would adhere to a target for uranium sales and transfers of no more than 10 percent of the annual U.S. requirements for nuclear fuel. The target was established in part to alleviate concerns raised by uranium industry officials that sales of uranium by DOE could harm the domestic uranium mining, conversion, and enrichment industries. Such concerns included a fear that sudden marked increases in the supply of uranium could depress prices. The targeted limit on uranium sales and transfers reflects DOE and uranium industry officials' concurrence that the industry could withstand, without adverse material impact, the addition to the market from DOE's uranium inventory of up to 10 percent of the U.S. demand for uranium in any year.

DOE's December 2008 plan estimated that U.S. nuclear fuel requirements would be about 19,250 metric tons of uranium annually from 2008 through 2010. According to industry analysts, requirements are likely to increase gradually to about 20,000 metric tons by 2013.[9] As shown in table 3, the total uranium DOE released to the market represented only about 5 percent of total U.S. demand in 2008 and 6 percent in 2009, significantly below the 10 percent target established by the plan.

DOE Plans to Release More Uranium into the Market Sooner Than Detailed in the Plan

Consistent with its 2008 plan, DOE has successfully kept its sales or transfers of uranium below the 10 percent target, but it has departed from other key provisions in its 2008 plan. For example, the plan scheduled uranium sales or transfers so that uranium would be released into the market gradually from 2009 through 2013. As shown in figure 1, DOE originally intended to increase the amount of uranium released year by year, from about 600 metric tons of uranium in 2008 to nearly 2,000 metric tons by 2013. But as a result of the uranium transactions with USEC and Fluor-B&W Portsmouth, which were announced after DOE's December 2008 plan, DOE is poised to release substantially more uranium faster than the plan stated.

Table 3. Amount of Uranium DOE Released or Plans to Release to the Market Annually, 2008-2013

	2008[a]	2009[a]	2010[a]	2011[b]	2012[b]	2013[b]
Estimated total U.S. commercial nuclear fuel requirements	19,250	19,250	19,250	19,450	19,590	20,430
Uranium sold, transferred, or planned for sale or transfer						
To American Assured Fuel Supply Program	57	88	47	44	94	0
To MOX Backup Inventory Program[c]	0	0	0	47	128	334
To Tennessee Valley Authority	982	828	126	127	0	0
To Portsmouth contractors for cleanup services	0	202	921	1,605	1605	1,350
Total	**1,039**[d,e]	**1118**[e]	**1,094**[e]	**1,823**	**1,827**	**1,684**
Percentage of annual U.S. nuclear fuel requirements	5	6	6	9	9	8

Source: GAO analysis of data from DOE and Energy Resources International, Inc.
Note: Quantities are expressed as metric tons of natural uranium; totals and percentages have been rounded.
[a] Numbers for 2008-2010 represent actual amounts of uranium released.
[b] Numbers for 2011-2013 represent the most recent DOE estimates.
[c] DOE's MOX [mixed oxide] Backup LEU [low-enriched uranium] Inventory Program down-blends highly enriched uranium to low-enriched uranium to be used as a backup fuel supply to utilities participating in DOE's MOX program for surplus plutonium disposition.
[d] The 2008 total excludes the equivalent of 10.4 metric tons of natural uranium that DOE released to a private firm for use as commercial reactor fuel in Ukraine. This "off-specification" uranium contained contaminants that made it unsuitable for use in U.S. commercial nuclear power reactors.
[e] The 2008 to 2010 totals exclude the equivalent of 90 metric tons of natural uranium that DOE transferred to research reactors. Commercial uranium enrichment companies do not produce uranium at the required enrichment level for use in these reactors; DOE therefore supplies fuel at the appropriate enrichment level.

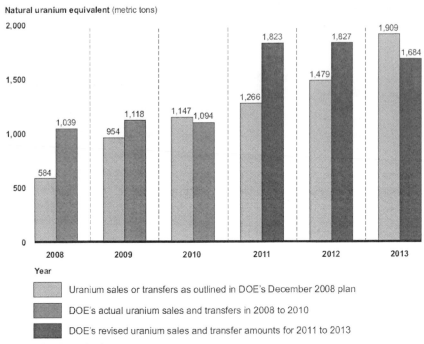

Source: GAO analysis.

Note: Bars for 2008-2010 compare DOE's 2008 management plan with actual amounts of uranium released to the commercial market. Bars for 2011 to 2013 compare amounts cited in DOE's 2008 management plan with DOE's current plan to sell or transfer uranium, revised as of December 2010.

Figure 1. Comparison of DOE's Planned Sales or Transfers, as Outlined in the December 2008 Excess Uranium Management Plan, with Actual and Expected Sales or Transfers, 2008-2013.

DOE's plan also stated that the department may sell or re-enrich up to 7,000 metric tons of depleted uranium from 2008 to 2017. We learned from DOE officials, however, that the department has no plans to release any inventory of depleted uranium in the near term. According to DOE officials, a key reason depleted uranium is not likely to be sold or re- enriched is concern that doing so would push total DOE uranium sales and transfers over the December 2008 plan's 10 percent target.

According to domestic uranium industry officials we interviewed, DOE's departure from its 2008 plan has created anxiety about how much further DOE might deviate from its plan in the future. In particular, industry officials were concerned that uncertainties about the quantities of uranium DOE might suddenly decide to sell or transfer could cause a fall in future uranium prices. Industry officials told us that this fear of declining prices discouraged potential investment in the industry, particularly in newer mining companies seeking to start production. Industry officials also said they feared that uncertainties about DOE's future plans would raise the costs of borrowing and of insurance coverage.

In discussions, DOE officials stated that the December 2008 uranium management plan was out of date soon after it was issued and that most of the plan's projected transfers from 2011 forward no longer reflected the department's present intentions. DOE officials told us that the department has begun work on updating the uranium management plan, but officials were unable to provide a date by which the update will be completed.

DOE'S URANIUM TRANSACTIONS WITH USEC WERE CONSISTENT WITH FEDERAL LAW GOVERNING URANIUM TRANSACTIONS BUT DID NOT COMPLY WITH FEDERAL FISCAL LAW

We found that DOE's uranium transactions with USEC constituted sales authorized under the USEC Privatization Act and that conditions the act requires before a uranium sale can be made were met.[10] We found, however, that by not depositing an amount equivalent to the proceeds from these transactions into the Treasury, DOE violated the miscellaneous receipts statute.[11]

DOE's Uranium Transactions with USEC Constituted Sales through an Agent

The Atomic Energy Act of 1954, as amended, gives DOE general authority under certain conditions to sell, lease, distribute, or otherwise make available source material,[12] including natural uranium. Congress, however, limited this authority in 1996 when it passed the USEC Privatization Act. This act prohibits the Secretary of Energy from transferring or selling any uranium except as consistent with the act's specific terms and conditions. The specific provision governing the material that DOE provided to USEC authorizes only sales of that material.

We found that from December 2009 through March 2011, DOE sold natural uranium into the market using USEC as its agent. DOE maintains that these transactions constituted barters with USEC, rather than sales by DOE using USEC as its agent, in that the transactions involved an exchange of services (environmental cleanup work) for materials (uranium). Our review of the substance of these transactions, however, showed that they were sales. A sale typically involves an exchange of goods or services for cash, and DOE in fact arranged for USEC to receive cash from the sale of federal uranium assets as compensation for services USEC provided to DOE. The transactions were thus sales executed through an agent—USEC. (Appendix III contains a detailed legal analysis of these issues.) Such sales are authorized by the USEC Privatization Act.[13] Because we found that the transactions were sales, we did not consider and did not decide whether barters are also authorized under the USEC Privatization Act.[14]

Two key factors demonstrate that DOE's transactions with USEC were sales through an agent, rather than barters: first, DOE had control over USEC's sales of the uranium, which was the property of the federal government, and second, and USEC sold the uranium for the benefit of the government and assumed no financial risk in the transaction.

According to USEC officials, USEC finalized the sales of uranium to third parties before it signed the contract modifications under which it agreed to conduct cleanup in exchange for the uranium. That is, USEC arranged for the sale of federal property; it did not sell its own property. DOE has stated that it did not control the sale of the uranium under the terms of the contract modifications with USEC, but because the uranium was marketed and sold before those contract modifications were made final, the terms of the contract modification did not govern the sale. Instead, DOE and USEC officials told us that they had an earlier, oral agreement for the valuation of the material under which USEC solicited buyers for federal uranium assets. During the term of this agreement, which led directly to sales of the uranium, DOE had the right to exercise control over USEC's actions as an agent.[15] Moreover, USEC sold the uranium primarily for DOE's benefit. USEC stated in its 2010 annual report to the U.S. Securities and Exchange Commission[16] that it never considered itself the owner of the uranium because the company assumed no risk in its sale and did not stand to earn a profit. USEC also stated in the report that the amount of work USEC was to provide under the cleanup contract depended on the net value of the uranium (minus transaction costs). If USEC had secured less value for the material, it would have done less work for DOE; it therefore did not stand to gain or lose on the uranium sales. The primary beneficiary of the transactions was DOE, which sought to structure the transactions to avoid the receipt of cash it was not authorized to retain and use to pay for cleanup at the Portsmouth facility.

That USEC acted as DOE's agent is also indicated by the value DOE received for the uranium (in terms of work to be performed by USEC), which was reduced by an amount equal to the transaction costs that USEC incurred in the sale of the uranium. In other words, DOE did not receive the gross value, or price, that USEC realized from the sale of the uranium but instead received value equal to the net proceeds of its sale.

USEC deducted from its valuation of the natural uranium transfer costs for such things as materials handling and a commission covering its sales management activities. For example, USEC deducted $825,000 in sales management fees, plus other transaction and transfer costs, from the value of the uranium involved in the transaction. A USEC official said that the sales management fees were for the time and expertise to collect offers, value the material, negotiate sales of the material, and execute book transfers of the material. In other words, USEC charged a commission against the value of the material. DOE officials stated that such transactional fees or costs are routinely part of any commodity transaction. We agree that such costs routinely figure into commodity transactions, but where those costs are incurred by the recipient and charged back to the seller, and where those costs include a commission, the transactions are most accurately understood as ones involving an agent. DOE has mischaracterized the transactions as barters, but it is not this mischaracterization that makes the transactions illegal. The transactions constituted sales, and sales—whether through an agent or not—are authorized by the USEC Privatization Act. Rather, DOE's legal violation occurred when it failed to deposit the value of the net proceeds into the Treasury as required by the miscellaneous receipts statute.

Conditions Required by the USEC Privatization Act Were Met, but Analysis of the Market Impact of the Uranium Transactions Was Inconclusive

For DOE to carry out sales under the USEC Privatization Act, three conditions must first be met.[17] First, the President must determine that the uranium intended for sale is not needed for national security. The uranium involved in DOE's transactions with USEC has been in DOE's inventory for over a decade. According to DOE, in that time this uranium has never been included in a nuclear weapons stockpile memorandum signed by the President, which identifies inventories of uranium for national defense needs. Because the uranium involved in DOE's transactions was not included in the most recent memorandum, the Nuclear Weapons Council—a joint Department of Defense and DOE organization established by Congress to manage the U.S. nuclear weapons stockpile—approved the release of the material for other purposes. Thus, the first condition was met.

Second, the USEC Privatization Act requires that the Secretary of Energy receive no less than fair market value for uranium sold. To ensure that this condition was met, DOE officials said they assessed USEC's proposed valuation of the uranium and considered the most recent average spot market prices and USEC's transfer costs. The department then issued a determination that USEC's valuation represented fair market value for the material. Although we did not conduct our own analysis as to whether the Secretary in fact received fair market value for the uranium, we do not dispute the department's determination that it met this requirement of the USEC Privatization Act.

Third, the act requires the Secretary of Energy to determine that proposed transactions will have no adverse material impact on the domestic uranium mining, conversion, and enrichment industries. To meet this requirement, DOE contracted with an energy research firm, Energy Resources International, which issued a market impact analysis in November 2009 that projected the potential market effects of planned uranium sales and transfers from the last quarter of calendar year 2009 through 2013.[18] The study took into consideration the five planned transactions for environmental cleanup at Portsmouth, as well as other planned transactions, including those between NNSA and the Tennessee Valley Authority and the American Assured Fuel Supply Program, among others.[19] The authors of the study stated that DOE's planned transactions would have no adverse material impact on uranium producers, and DOE issued the required determination on the basis of this study. Thus, the third condition under the USEC Privatization Act was met.

Nevertheless, our review found the results of the market impact analysis to be inconclusive. The economic model developed by Energy Resources International analyzed market impact for the term market and included assumptions about supply-and-demand characteristics that represent the long-term, rather than the spot market, even though DOE, industry experts, and Energy Resources International analysts themselves agreed that DOE uranium transactions would have the potential to affect the spot market most.[20] Furthermore, the study stated that long-term prices are more relevant to investment decisions by the industry. In fact, in a subsequent study issued in

December 2010 to account for additional DOE transactions beginning in 2011, Energy Resources International expanded its analysis to include the price impact of the transfers on the spot market, which it had previously characterized as too difficult to assess.[21]

The new study included an econometric model to evaluate the price impact in the spot market, but we found that it too was inconclusive.[22] In particular, the econometric model used historic data on price, quantity supplied, and quantity demanded and did not identify and evaluate the effects of other factors that could also affect the behavior of uranium spot prices. These factors could include market participants' expectations about future uranium supply and demand, as well as their expectations of future levels of uranium inventories. In addition, because the details about uranium sales through both long-term contracts and the spot market are typically considered business proprietary information, data about expected future uranium supply and demand are usually not available and thus difficult or impossible to adequately model. A change in the price of competing energy resources, such as oil and coal, could also affect uranium spot prices. Changes in the prices of related minerals found in tandem with uranium, such as gold, copper, and vanadium, can also affect uranium spot prices. Specifically, a high market price for gold, copper, vanadium may encourage uranium exploration and production. Furthermore, domestic and international political and economic events or natural disasters—such as the March 2011 earthquake, tsunami, and subsequent nuclear accident in Japan—can affect uranium spot prices.

Because the econometric model used was not able to evaluate any of these factors, its estimate of the change in the spot market price of uranium caused by an isolated event would be inconclusive. We agree, as Energy Resources International noted in its study, that it is difficult to predict a specific change in the spot market price due to one particular future event, such as a DOE uranium transaction.

DOE Violated the Miscellaneous Receipts Statute by Not Depositing the Value of Net Proceeds from Uranium Transactions with USEC into the Treasury

DOE violated the miscellaneous receipts statute in handling the proceeds of its sales of uranium through USEC. This statute requires that "an official or agent of the Government receiving money for the Government from any source shall deposit the money in the Treasury as soon as practicable without deduction for any charge or claim."[23] Generally, a federal agency may not operate beyond the level that it can finance with its annual appropriation without specific congressional authorization. For an agency to keep money that has not been appropriated is to undercut Congress's constitutional power of the purse.[24]

In providing uranium to USEC for sale to a third party and allowing USEC to keep the proceeds, DOE constructively received money for the government and improperly extended its reach beyond the operating level that it was otherwise authorized to achieve through its congressional appropriation. DOE officials readily acknowledged that if the department had sold the uranium directly into the market and received cash, it would have had to deposit that cash into the Treasury. DOE officials also acknowledged that it structured its transactions with USEC the way it did so as to avoid having to deposit the proceeds of a sale into the Treasury. DOE said that without this mechanism, it would not have been able to fund the accelerated cleanup at Portsmouth. In DOE's view, however, because it received no cash in these transactions, it was not required to deposit any proceeds into the Treasury.

We disagree with DOE's conclusion—that, because it received no direct cash for its uranium, it was not subject to the miscellaneous receipts statute—for the same reasons that we found similar actions by DOE in 2006, also involving use of USEC as its sales agent, to violate this law.[25] It is a well-understood principle of law that what cannot be done directly cannot be done indirectly.[26] An agency that lacks authority to retain and use amounts that it receives directly cannot circumvent its lack of authority by engaging a contractor or, as here, a sales agent to indirectly receive, retain, and use the funds.[27] To the extent that Congress sees merit in the additional cleanup work that DOE states is needed at its facilities, it could provide DOE with explicit authority to barter uranium, as well as authority to receive and retain funding from the department's barters, transfers, and sales of uranium.

CONCLUSION

One purpose of DOE's December 2008 uranium management plan was to reassure the domestic uranium industry that the department would refrain from suddenly releasing unanticipated amounts of uranium into the market. But by announcing, 8 months after issuing its plan, uranium transactions that were not envisioned in the plan, DOE introduced additional uncertainty into that market. Partly as a result of the department's actions, the domestic uranium producers we interviewed fear the consequences of future transactions in which the department may engage. Without an accurate, updated plan that clearly details DOE's future uranium activities and the circumstances under which departmental plans could change, companies in the domestic uranium industry cannot adequately anticipate the department's actions and take steps to mitigate the consequences of those actions.

Federal law authorizes DOE to dispose of its excess uranium by selling it directly on the open market and depositing the proceeds in the Treasury. According to DOE officials with whom we spoke, however, DOE has no incentive to do so because the department would be unable to use the proceeds for its own cleanup priorities without specific congressional authorization. Nevertheless, our review indicates that DOE's uranium transactions with USEC constituted sales and that USEC served as the department's sales agent. Even though DOE did not directly receive cash for its uranium, in our view the transactions constituted sales, and thus the department was required to deposit an amount equal to the value of the uranium into the Treasury. By not doing so, DOE has inappropriately circumvented the power of the purse granted to Congress under the Constitution and violated the miscellaneous receipts statute. We do not question the need to decontaminate and decommission DOE's uranium enrichment facilities. If, however, the department cannot finance these cleanup activities without additional funding, it is the prerogative of Congress, not DOE, to make the necessary funding available.

RECOMMENDATION FOR EXECUTIVE ACTION

To improve DOE's management of its excess uranium inventories, we recommend that the Secretary of Energy update the December 2008 "Excess Uranium Inventory Management Plan" to more accurately reflect DOE's plans for marketing its uranium.

MATTER FOR CONGRESSIONAL CONSIDERATION

If Congress sees merit in using proceeds from the barter, transfer, or sale of federal uranium assets to pay for environmental cleanup of uranium enrichment facilities, it should consider:

- providing DOE with explicit authority to barter excess uranium and to retain the proceeds from barters, transfers, or sales or
- directing DOE to sell federal uranium assets for cash and directing that collected proceeds be made available for obligation only to the extent and in the amount provided in advance in appropriations acts for necessary expenses in decontaminating and decommissioning uranium facilities and directing DOE to deposit into the Treasury any excess over what is appropriated.

AGENCY COMMENTS AND OUR EVALUATION

We provided a draft of this report to DOE for comment. In its written comments, DOE agreed with our recommendation to update its excess uranium management plan but disagreed that the department violated federal fiscal law.

In general, DOE's comments focused on our finding that DOE's uranium transactions constituted sales through an agent. Specifically, DOE commented that its transfer of uranium to USEC was a barter, exchanging uranium assets for environmental cleanup, and that USEC was not a sales agent for the department. Therefore, according to DOE, the department did not violate the miscellaneous receipt statute. DOE stated that no authorized official signed a written agreement with USEC under which the company would sell uranium for DOE, nor could the department be bound by an oral agreement. DOE stated that the contract modifications under which USEC agreed to conduct cleanup in exchange for uranium did not include any language indicating USEC should obtain offers for DOE uranium or otherwise serve as DOE's sales agent. In DOE's view, we should not have considered any evidence other than the written contract modifications between DOE and USEC. DOE also disagreed with our statement that USEC faced no risk of loss in its sale of the uranium and that DOE paid a commission to USEC for its sale of the uranium. In addition, DOE disagreed that it entered into the transactions with USEC specifically to avoid receiving cash, contrary to what USEC and DOE officials explicitly told us. Instead, DOE stated the purpose of the transactions was to achieve accelerated cleanup of the Portsmouth site, which would help create or retain jobs at the site and save the federal government money in long-term maintenance costs. DOE also disagreed with our estimate of the value of the department's depleted uranium tails and provided updated data on the department's actual and planned uranium sales and transfers.

DOE's comments do not undermine our conclusion that the department violated the miscellaneous receipts statute. DOE arranged for USEC to receive cash from the sales of federal uranium as compensation for cleanup activities that DOE would otherwise have had to pay for out of its appropriated funds. Rather than address this fact, DOE reasserts its position that the transactions constituted barters, not sales through an agent. DOE's argument is misplaced, however. Whether the transactions were barters or sales goes mainly to the question of whether DOE was authorized to engage in the transactions at all under the USEC Privatization Act, and we found that the transactions were authorized as sales.[28] As we noted in our report, that the transactions were sales and not barters is also significant to the question of whether DOE complied with the miscellaneous receipts statute, but only in that DOE did not deposit the net proceeds from its sales into the Treasury. The department does not refute, however, the central tenet behind our conclusion that it violated the miscellaneous receipts statute. It asserts that because it did not receive any actual cash in the transaction, it did not have to deposit any money into the Treasury. As we noted in our draft report, GAO and the courts have found in a number of instances that an entity does not have to receive actual cash to trigger a responsibility to deposit money into the Treasury.

DOE's comments also do not refute our finding that its transactions with USEC were sales through an agent. DOE focuses on the lack of a written agreement between the department and USEC that establishes the company as DOE's agent. We agree that no written agreement exists authorizing USEC to value DOE's uranium assets. Nevertheless, DOE has acknowledged the existence of an oral agreement, and whether DOE could be bound to act under such an agreement is not relevant to the present analysis. The fact remains that DOE requested USEC's valuation of the uranium, which it knew to be based on the solicitation of firm offers for the material and which led directly to the uranium's sale. Further, it was necessary and appropriate to look to evidence other than the contract modifications because the contract modifications do not cover valuation of the uranium.

Our review, therefore, appropriately examined the process USEC and DOE used to establish the uranium's value before the contract modifications were signed. Our review of this process also established that USEC in fact faced no risk of loss in its sale of the uranium because it sold the uranium *before* agreeing on how much work it would do in exchange for the uranium. In addition, DOE did pay a commission to USEC under the common definition of the term, that is, "a fee paid to an agent or employee for transacting a piece of business or performing a service."[29] DOE acknowledges that it paid a "sales management fee" to USEC. We see no distinction between such a fee and a commission. Further, we do not dispute DOE's contention that the overall purpose of accelerating the Portsmouth cleanup work may have been to save on long-term site maintenance costs and protect local employment, but DOE officials repeatedly told us that the department chose to pay for this project in the manner it did specifically to avoid the receipt of cash. DOE provided no other reason why it would seek to barter uranium rather than sell it. We therefore conclude that DOE manipulated the disposition of federal assets to avoid the payment of proceeds for those assets into the federal Treasury. Doing so violated the miscellaneous receipts statute.

With regard to our estimate of the value of DOE's depleted uranium tails, DOE stated that the draft report did not include any source or backup information for our $4.2 billion estimate of the tails' value. DOE's statement is incorrect. The draft report cited our June 2011 report that explained in detail how we developed our estimate. Specifically, our estimate is based on a model we previously developed that uses standard formulas to estimate how much enriched uranium and tails can be produced from a given amount of uranium and enrichment services. The model employs price data obtained from nuclear industry trade publications. Such data are commonly used to estimate the market price for uranium. We agree with DOE that our estimate of the tails' value does not include the additional costs that may be incurred processing tails stored in deteriorating cylinders, addressing the poor quality of some material, or packaging and transporting the material. Our estimate omits these costs because they are unknown. DOE is mistaken, however, in stating that our estimate does not include the costs of production. Our model includes the cost of enrichment services in its estimate of the tails' net value. Nevertheless, as our June 2011 report and the draft report noted, our estimate is very sensitive to changing uranium prices, as well as to the availability of sufficient enrichment capacity. Uranium prices are volatile, and a sharp rise or fall can greatly affect the value of uranium tails. Any estimates of the value of DOE's tails are therefore subject to great uncertainty.

Finally, after we received the department's comments on our draft report, DOE officials provided additional updated data on the department's actual and planned uranium sales and transfers. We revised the report accordingly to reflect the most current data DOE provided to us.

Gene Aloise
Director, Natural Resources and Environment

Susan D. Sawtelle
Managing Associate General Counsel

APPENDIX I. SCOPE AND METHODOLOGY

To identify the Department of Energy's (DOE) transactions involving excess uranium used to pay for accelerated cleanup work at the Portsmouth Gaseous Diffusion Plant, we obtained department summary data drawn from the Nuclear Materials Management and Safeguard System regarding all sales and transfers of uranium from January 1, 2008, through June 30, 2011. To identify specific transactions involving natural uranium during this time frame, we also obtained and reviewed individual nuclear materials transaction reports, which detailed the change of uranium ownership from DOE to the United States Enrichment Corporation (USEC) and to Fluor-B&W Portsmouth. We obtained information on the value of these transactions and the services paid for by these transactions by reviewing uranium valuation documents from USEC and Fluor-B&W Portsmouth, as well as the relevant DOE contracts or contract modifications related to the transactions. To further our understanding of these transactions and to determine DOE's future plans to sell or transfer uranium, we interviewed DOE nuclear materials management officials from the National Nuclear Security Administration (NNSA), the Office of Nuclear Energy, and the Office of Environmental Management. We also met with or interviewed by phone knowledgeable USEC officials at the Paducah Gaseous Diffusion Plant in Kentucky and Fluor-B&W Portsmouth officials at the Portsmouth Gaseous Diffusion Plant in Ohio. We did not determine the accuracy of DOE's uranium inventory data or specifically verify the amount of uranium physically transferred from DOE to other entities, including USEC and Fluor-B&W Portsmouth. We instead reviewed extensive department guidance regarding the Nuclear Materials Management and Safeguard System, including the Nuclear Materials Control and Accountability System, which tracks the character, location, and transfer of all federal inventories of nuclear materials, including uranium. Associated documentation indicates that an extensive program exists to ensure the accuracy of information on the nuclear materials inventory, but we nevertheless reviewed recent assessments of key databases that make up the nuclear materials management system. No material weaknesses were reported. We therefore determined that uranium inventory data drawn from these systems were sufficiently reliable for purposes of this report.

To determine the extent to which DOE's natural uranium transactions were consistent with DOE's "Excess Uranium Inventory Management Plan" issued in 2008, we compared key provisions of the plan to DOE's specific activities to manage its uranium inventory. To develop an understanding of DOE's uranium management activities, we interviewed DOE officials at the Portsmouth/Paducah Project Office in Lexington, Kentucky, which has managed the recent uranium transactions, as well as the DOE contracting officers responsible for negotiating and executing federal contracts for cleanup services. To develop an understanding of the impact that DOE's uranium transactions might have on the market for uranium products, we also interviewed a wide range of uranium industry representatives. These representatives included officials from uranium trade associations; startup and established mining companies; ConverDyn's conversion facility in Metropolis, Illinois; and USEC's gaseous diffusion enrichment plant in Paducah, Kentucky. We also interviewed officials from selected utility companies operating commercial nuclear power plants, commodities brokers and traders, and market analysts. We visited two mining operations, a Cameco corporation "in situ" uranium mine at Smith Ranch, Wyoming, and the Denison Mines corporation underground mine and uranium milling facility near Blanding, Utah.

Finally, to determine the extent to which DOE's uranium transactions were consistent with applicable federal law, we reviewed requirements of the Atomic Energy Act,[30] the USEC Privatization Act[31] and the miscellaneous receipts statute.[32] We obtained and reviewed internal DOE documentation authorizing uranium transactions and changing ownership of cylinders containing natural uranium to USEC and to Fluor-B&W Portsmouth. We reviewed market impact analyses prepared by Energy Resources International, Inc., under contract with DOE; internal documents certifying that DOE would receive fair market value for its natural uranium; and secretarial determinations that uranium transactions would have no adverse impact on the uranium market and that the uranium was not needed for national security purposes. For information on how the uranium transactions were documented for accounting purposes, we also reviewed USEC's annual 10-K report to the Securities and Exchange Commission and interviewed USEC and Fluor-B&W Portsmouth business and accounting officials.

We conducted this performance audit from November 2010 through September 2011, in accordance with generally accepted government auditing standards. Those standards require that we plan and perform the audit to obtain sufficient, appropriate evidence to provide a reasonable basis for our findings and conclusions based on our audit objectives. We believe that the evidence obtained provides a reasonable basis for our findings and conclusions based on our audit objectives.

APPENDIX II. THE NUCLEAR FUEL CYCLE

1. Finding Uranium Deposits

Unlike coal, which forms continuous seams in rock, uranium forms discrete, concentrated deposits distributed like the specks in blue cheese. Uranium can be found by detecting the presence of radioactivity from the air, from the earth's surface, or by excavation.

Source: U.S. Geological Survey.

Uranium ore

2. Uranium Mining Regulation and Startup

The uranium mining industry is regulated by various federal and state authorities. To bring a mine into production takes 8 to 10 years and costs many millions of dollars.

The cost to bring a conventional open-pit or underground mine on line can be up to $400 million, while an "in situ" mine, which extracts minerals from an underground aquifer, costs about $100 million.

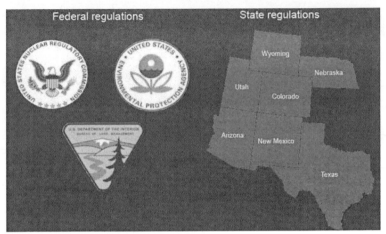

Sources: GAO; Map Resources (map).

3. Conventional Mining

Conventional open-pit mining gains access to ore by using explosives to remove surface material. If the uranium is too far below the surface, tunnels and shafts are dug to reach and extract the ore. Broken ore is then sent to a processing mill.

At the mill, the ore is crushed, ground, and then fed to a leaching system that uses resin and chemicals to separate uranium from the ore. The resulting yellow slurry—called "yellowcake"⬤ —is washed, dried, and sold to utility customers.

Interactive features: Roll your mouse ⬤ over to see yellowcake.

Source: U.S. Department of Energy.

Open-pit uranium mine.

4. Mining by In Situ Recovery

In situ mineral recovery circulates naturally occurring groundwater through uranium deposits in porous sandstone. At the surface, the uranium is treated to separate it from the water and then dried. The resulting yellowcake is sold to utility customers.

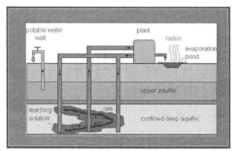

Source: World Information Service on Energy Uranium Project.

In situ mineral recovery.

5. Converting Uranium

The uranium in yellowcake is heated and combined with other gases to produce uranium hexafluoride, a gas. Once cooled, uranium hexafluoride crystallizes and becomes a solid, which can be easily shipped in cylinders to a uranium enrichment plant.

Interactive features: Roll your mouse over to see uranium hexafluoride crystals.

Source: ConverDyn.

Inside ConverDyn's conversion plant.

6. Department of Energy Inventory of Uranium Hexafluoride

The Department of Energy oversees a substantial supply of uranium hexafluoride cylinders left over from prior nuclear weapons programs or received under U.S. nuclear nonproliferation agreements with the Russian Federation.

The department has occasionally sold or transferred this uranium, most recently to accelerate cleanup of the Portsmouth Gaseous Diffusion Plant near Piketon, Ohio.

Source: U.S. Department of Energy.

The Department of Energy's uranium hexafluoride cylinders.

7. Uranium Enrichment

Commercial nuclear reactors in the United States require fuel consisting of at least 3 percent concentration of uranium-235. Uranium hexafluoride, the gaseous form of natural uranium, contains a concentration of only 0.71 percent uranium-235 and therefore requires enrichment before it can be used as fuel. In the United States, enrichment is done primarily by means of gaseous diffusion and gas centrifuge.

Source: Nuclear Regulatory Commission.

Nuclear power plant.

8. Enrichment by Gaseous Diffusion

Enriching uranium through gaseous diffusion repeatedly forces uranium hexafluoride under pressure through porous membranes, separating the isotope uranium-235 from uranium-238. The gas must be processed through as many as 1,400 stages to achieve a concentration of 3 percent uranium-235.

Interactive features: Roll your mouse ● over to see the gaseous diffusion stage.

Source: U.S. Department of Energy.

Gaseous diffusion equipment.

9. Enrichment by Gas Centrifuge

Enriching uranium with a gas centrifuge involves spinning uranium hexafluoride gas at high speed in a series of cylinders to separate uranium-235 from uranium-238. Centrifuge technology requires only 10 to 20 stages and a fraction of the energy required for gaseous diffusion.

Source: Urenco LTD.

Bank of centrifuges.

10. Fuel fabrication

To fabricate fuel, enriched uranium hexafluoride gas is combined with other elements to form a uranium dioxide powder, which is compressed, formed into pellets, and then sealed into long metal tubes to form fuel rods. These rods are bundled to create a fuel assembly.

Depending on the reactor type, about 179 to 264 fuel rods are required for each fuel assembly; a typical reactor core holds 121 to 193 fuel assemblies.

Interactive features: Roll your mouse over bubble to see fuel pellet.

Source: Nuclear Regulatory Commission.

Fuel assemblies.

APPENDIX III. LEGAL ANALYSIS OF DOE'S STRATEGY TO FINANCE USEC'S CLEANUP WORK AT THE PORTSMOUTH GASEOUS DIFFUSION PLANT

Introduction and Summary of Conclusions

As part of GAO's review of DOE's overall uranium management plan, we examined what DOE referred to as a series of "barter arrangements" between DOE and USEC for accelerated cleanup services at the Portsmouth Gaseous Diffusion Plant. Specifically, we examined the consistency of these transactions with federal law governing uranium transactions and the disposition of government assets.

We found that DOE's transactions constituted sales of uranium, which were authorized under the USEC Privatization Act but violated the miscellaneous receipts statute because DOE failed to deposit the value of the net proceeds into the Treasury. We came to the same conclusion in 2006 in analyzing a similar series of transactions between DOE and USEC. In particular, although DOE has characterized its most recent transactions with USEC as "barters," they are more accurately characterized as sales of uranium into the market, with USEC acting as DOE's sales agent. The miscellaneous receipts statute requires government officials who receive money for the government to deposit the money into the Treasury. Although DOE did not receive cash from the sale of federal uranium assets, it allowed USEC to receive and keep cash from the sales. Because DOE was not authorized to keep the sale proceeds, the department also was not authorized to engage USEC to receive them. The current transactions differ in some superficial respects from the 2006 transactions, but the core substance is the same, and, as DOE told us, in this case it intentionally structured the disposition of federal assets to avoid payment of the proceeds for those assets into the federal Treasury.

Analysis

DOE's Uranium Transactions with USEC Were Sales Authorized by the USEC Privatization Act

Under the Atomic Energy Act of 1954, as amended,[33] DOE has general authority to sell, lease, distribute, or otherwise make available source material, including natural uranium, under certain conditions to licensed entities. Congress limited this general authority in 1996, however, in the USEC Privatization Act.[34] Section 3 112(a) of this act explicitly prohibits DOE from selling or transferring "any uranium" except as "consistent with" section 3112. The remaining provisions of section 3112 then specify the conditions under which DOE may sell or transfer various types of natural and enriched uranium. Section 3112(b) covers uranium transferred to DOE under the US-Russia Highly Enriched Uranium Purchase Agreement in 1995 and 1996. Section 31 12(c) covers natural and enriched uranium transferred before 1998 to USEC without charge as part of its privatization. Section 3112(e) covers transfers of enriched uranium to federal, state, and local agencies; nonprofit, charitable, or educational institutions; and others. Section 3112(d)(1) covers natural and low-enriched uranium sold from DOE's inventory that is not otherwise covered under sections 3112(b), (c), or (e). According to DOE, the uranium subject to the 2009-2011 transactions with USEC was natural uranium from DOE's inventory. It therefore does not fall into any of the categories covered by sections 3112(b), (c), or (e) and is thus covered by section 3112(d)(1).[35] Because section 3112(d)(1) only authorizes sales, DOE's transactions with USEC must be sales or else be prohibited by the USEC Privatization Act.

According to DOE, its transactions with USEC constituted barters—an exchange of goods (natural uranium) for services (accelerated cleanup services at the Portsmouth Gaseous Diffusion Plant) authorized by the Atomic Energy Act—and are not "inconsistent with" the USEC Privatization Act. DOE declined to explain to us whether and how barters authorized under the Atomic Energy Act also constitute sales authorized by the USEC Privatization Act. DOE instead stressed that because it relies on its broad Atomic Energy Act authority to dispose of source material, the distinction between barters and sales is not relevant. Specifically, in DOE's view, the USEC Privatization Act does not affect its authority under the Atomic Energy Act to engage in transactions involving uranium but simply establishes additional conditions that apply to the exercise of its authority under this act.[36] Because we found that the current transactions in question were sales (through an agent) of uranium, and because all such sales are governed by the USEC Privatization Act, we need not and did not address whether barters are authorized under this act.

In this report we found, as we did in analyzing similar transactions in 2006, that DOE's transactions with USEC constituted sales authorized by section 31 12(d)(1) of the USEC Privatization Act—but through USEC as agent, rather than to USEC as buyer.[37] DOE and USEC had different views about the nature of their relationship with respect to the most recent transactions. DOE told us that it bartered federal uranium assets for cleanup services with USEC and did not employ USEC as an agent to sell the uranium to third parties. By contrast, a USEC official told us that USEC did act as DOE's sales agent and in its 2010 annual report to the U.S. Securities and Exchange Commission[38] stated that USEC never owned the material because it did not stand to make a profit or loss from the uranium sale. Labels that parties ascribe to their roles are not controlling as to whether a principal-agent relationship exists, however. That relationship is determined by considering four key characteristics and looking to the substance of the transaction as a whole, with no single characteristic being determinative.[39] The four characteristics of a sales agency arrangement are (1) one entity delivers goods to another; (2) the other entity is to sell the goods not as his own property but as the property of and for the benefit of another, with the first entity remaining the owner of the goods; (3) the first entity has the right to control the sale, fix the price and terms, and recall the goods; and (4) the first entity has the right to demand and receive proceeds of the goods when sold, minus the agent's commission.[40] The series of transactions between DOE and USEC exhibited the last three of these four characteristics, and the first, delivery of the goods, is not applicable to uranium.[41] Thus, taken as a whole, the DOE-USEC series of transactions indicates that the relationship was functionally one of agency, with DOE as the principal and USEC as the agent.

First, USEC sold uranium that was the property of the federal government primarily for the benefit of the government. According to USEC officials, USEC finalized the sales of the uranium to third parties before it signed the contract modifications with DOE under which it agreed to conduct cleanup in exchange for the uranium.[42] USEC arranged for the sale of federal property; it did not sell its own property. This point is underscored by USEC's 10-K report, in which it states that it did not consider itself to be the owner of the material.[43] USEC also sold the uranium primarily for DOE's benefit: USEC's 10-K states that USEC assumed no risk in the sale and did not stand to make any profit because the amount of work USEC was to provide under the cleanup contract was dependent on the net value of the uranium. USEC set the value of the uranium on the basis of offers it received for the uranium, the highest of which it subsequently accepted and translated into sales. If USEC had secured less value for the material, it would have done less work for DOE. The only benefit of the "barter" transaction accrued to DOE: as DOE officials told us, by purportedly structuring the transactions as barters, DOE sought to avoid receiving cash, which it would have had to deposit into the Treasury. USEC kept the proceeds of the sale and used them for the cleanup services it provided at the Portsmouth facility but became entitled to the value of the uranium only after it signed the contract modifications to furnish cleanup services in exchange for that value. Those proceeds, therefore, cannot be said to be a benefit of the transaction that resulted in the sale of the uranium. The contract modifications purported to transfer title to the uranium to USEC, but at the time the contract modifications were signed, the uranium had already been sold. To the extent that title did actually pass through USEC, it could only have been to facilitate further transfers to the ultimate buyers.[44]

Second, DOE had the right to control the sale of the uranium. DOE stated that it did not control the sale of the uranium under the terms of the contract modifications with USEC but, rather, bartered federal uranium assets to USEC in exchange for cleanup services. DOE also stated that USEC was subsequently free to sell the uranium at any time it wished. The uranium was marketed and sold before the contract modifications were executed, however, so the terms of those contract modifications are not relevant in evaluating the control that DOE did or did not exercise over the sale. Instead, DOE and USEC officials told us that they had an oral agreement for the valuation of the material before the contract modifications were signed. DOE stated that it did not specifically authorize, require, or request USEC to solicit offers for the uranium but acknowledged that it requested USEC's valuation of the uranium, which it knew was to be based on the solicitation of firm offers for the material. During the term of this agreement, which led directly to sale of the uranium, DOE had the right to exercise control over USEC's actions as agent.

Moreover, although DOE officials stated that they did not know whether or when USEC in fact sold the material, a USEC official told us that a DOE official knew that USEC was seeking to finalize sales contracts with the highest bidders for the uranium and in fact encouraged USEC to finalize the sales quickly so that the contract modifications could be signed. In addition, two of the letters that USEC sent to DOE to establish the value of the uranium on the basis of offers received refer to the material as already sold.[45] These facts indicate that DOE was, or should have been, aware that the material was being sold before finalization of its "barter" agreement, while the material was still subject to DOE's control, and that DOE at least assented to, and may have explicitly authorized, the sales.

That DOE controlled the price obtained from the sales is also evinced by the fact that the valuation process, over which DOE had approval, was tied up with the sales process. USEC submitted its valuation of the uranium to DOE for approval for two reasons: (1) to determine the amount of work that USEC would be required to perform in exchange for that value and (2) to enable DOE to determine that it would receive fair market value for the material. Receipt of no less than fair market value is a condition required by the USEC Privatization Act before the sale of uranium.[46] As USEC stated in a series of letters to DOE establishing the value of the uranium, USEC felt that actual bids represented a more realistic value than mere consultation of spot market prices at the time of the sale. Soliciting firm offers for the material may have provided a realistic valuation of the material, but the same process also constituted USEC's first step in selling federally owned uranium on DOE's behalf. Further, this step was taken with DOE's knowledge and approval, including its specific approval of the price to be attained.[47]

Third, the value that DOE received for the uranium, in terms of work to be performed by USEC, was reduced by an amount equal to the transaction costs that USEC incurred in the sale of the uranium. In other words, DOE did not receive the gross value, or price, that USEC realized from the sale of the uranium but instead received value equal to the net proceeds of its sale. USEC deducted its transaction costs from the value it attributed to the uranium, and DOE approved that net value as the fair market value of the material. The value USEC attributed to the uranium was also the price received from its buyers, and the fact that costs were deducted from the value means that the value DOE received equaled the net proceeds of the sale to a third party from its agent, USEC, rather than the price of the sale from USEC as buyer.

Furthermore, the value of the uranium was decreased to account for USEC's "sales management fee" in addition to USEC's other transaction costs. USEC clearly labeled these amounts as sales management fees in its valuation letters for DOE approval, and DOE did in fact approve the net valuations. A USEC official told us that the sales management fee represented USEC's fee for brokering the material, USEC's fee for negotiating the actual sales of the material, and USEC's costs associated with arranging book transfers of the material. In other words, USEC charged a commission against the value of the material. DOE has stated that such transactional fees or costs are routinely part of any commodity transaction. We agree that such costs routinely figure into commodity transactions, but where those costs are incurred by the recipient and charged back to the seller, and where those costs include a commission, they indicate a transaction involving an agent.

In sum, DOE's uranium transactions with USEC, viewed as a whole, constituted sales through an agent rather than barters. USEC arranged for the sale of federal uranium assets while the uranium was still federal property. The only party that benefited from the sale was DOE. USEC deducted its transactions costs, as well as a commission, from the value of the uranium. These are all characteristics of sales agency rather than barter and resale. Even assuming some ambiguity in how these facts and circumstances should be characterized—agency or sale—courts have long found against the party whose mixed motives created the ambiguity.[48] In this case, any mixed motives are attributable to DOE. DOE's acknowledged objectives were to accomplish the cleanup work and avoid using appropriated funds to do so. It was motivated to structure the uranium transactions as purported barters so that it would not receive cash that it would have to deposit into the Treasury. At the same time, it was motivated to provide an arrangement acceptable to USEC so that the cleanup work could be accomplished. USEC's sole motivation was to minimize the risks inherent in the transaction. USEC officials told us they only accepted uranium as payment for cleanup services because they did not believe that DOE could finance the cleanup work with cash (i.e., appropriated funds), and they wanted the cleanup work to proceed to keep the skilled employees at Portsmouth working until USEC could open its new gas centrifuge enrichment facility there. Thus, USEC accepted the arrangement DOE offered, but only after it had found buyers for DOE's uranium, so the time USEC held the uranium and USEC's exposure to swings in the uranium market would be minimized. USEC was willing to take DOE's uranium only in a manner that made it DOE's sales agent. Although DOE did not specifically ask USEC to deal with the uranium in this way, DOE knew what actions USEC was taking and approved of the steps USEC took along the way. The true nature and effect of this arrangement was that USEC served as DOE's agent in selling federal uranium assets into the market.

DOE Violated the Miscellaneous Receipts Statute by Not Depositing the Value of Net Proceeds from Uranium Transactions with USEC into the Treasury

Our present review found, as did our analysis of similar transactions in 2006, that DOE did not comply with the miscellaneous receipts statute because it did not deposit the proceeds from sale of its uranium into the Treasury. Under the miscellaneous receipts statute, "an official or agent of the Government receiving money for the Government from any source shall deposit the money in the Treasury as soon as practicable without deduction for any charge or claim."[49] As a general proposition, a federal agency may not augment its appropriations from Congress without specific statutory authority. [50] When Congress makes an annual appropriation to an agency, it is also establishing an authorized program level. In other words, Congress is telling the agency that it cannot operate beyond the level it can finance under its appropriation. To permit an agency to operate beyond this level, with funds derived from some other source without specific congressional approval, would amount to a usurpation of Congress's constitutional prerogative to appropriate funds. Restated, the objective of the rule against augmentation of appropriations is to prevent a government agency from undercutting Congress's constitutional "power of the purse" by circuitously exceeding the amount Congress has appropriated for that activity. For an agency to keep money that has not been appropriated by Congress is to augment its appropriation.

In providing uranium to USEC for sale to a third party and allowing USEC to keep the proceeds, DOE constructively received money for the government. DOE used the proceeds of the sale to fund activities that the department would otherwise have had to pay for out of its appropriation. By allowing USEC to retain the cash proceeds from the sale of federal uranium, DOE improperly extended its reach beyond the operating level that it was otherwise authorized to achieve through its congressional appropriation. DOE readily acknowledged to us that if it had sold its uranium directly into the market and received cash, it would have had to deposit that cash into the Treasury. DOE officials also told us that they structured the transactions with USEC as they did to avoid having to deposit the proceeds of a sale into the Treasury. DOE stated that because it received no cash in this transaction, it was not required to deposit any proceeds into the Treasury. We disagree with DOE's conclusion. It is a fundamental principle of law that what cannot be done directly cannot be done indirectly.[51] An agency that lacks the authority to retain and use amounts that it receives directly cannot circumvent its lack of authority by engaging a contractor or, as here, a sales agent to indirectly receive, retain, and use the funds.[52] In similar circumstances, the courts and we have recognized that a contractor constructively receiving money for a federal agency is not free of the requirement of the miscellaneous receipts statute: that funds received for the use of the United States be deposited in the Treasury.[53] We have also found that a federal agency receives money under the miscellaneous receipts statute if the receipts are to cover the expenses of the government or to pay government obligations.[54] Here, USEC received money for DOE. The uranium belonged to DOE when USEC arranged for its sale, but instead of passing the cash proceeds back to DOE, USEC was allowed to keep the cash as compensation for work under its cleanup contract—work for which it was DOE's responsibility to pay.

Finally, we examined whether DOE's set of transactions with USEC could be characterized as a no-cost contract. In a no-cost contract, a contractor provides a service to the government, but the government has no financial liability to the contractor and the contractor has no expectation of payment from the government. For example, in a case in which the General Services Administration contracted for real estate brokerage services and brokers were compensated not by the agency but through commissions received from landlords, we found that these contracts were no-cost contracts that did not violate the miscellaneous receipts statute.[55] The General Services Administration did not augment its appropriation by accepting services without payment, however, because it had no financial liability to the brokers; the common industry practice was for those brokers to receive their compensation from third parties. But the transactions between DOE and USEC were not comparable. In this case, DOE incurred a cost: it paid a total of

$194.3 million in federal uranium assets for accelerated cleanup services. It allowed USEC to retain cash from the sale of these assets as compensation for services USEC provided to DOE, services for which DOE would otherwise have had to pay out of its appropriated funds. Thus DOE, unlike the General Services Administration, augmented its appropriation.[56]

Conclusion

Transactions that DOE characterized as "barters" between itself and USEC, whereby federal uranium assets were used to compensate USEC for cleanup services at the Portsmouth Gaseous Diffusion Plant, are more accurately characterized as sales of uranium into the market with USEC acting as DOE's sales agent. Such sales complied with the USEC Privatization Act, but DOE violated the miscellaneous receipts statute when it did not deposit the value of the net proceeds of these sales into the Treasury. The fact that DOE did not receive any actual cash from the sales is irrelevant. DOE arranged for USEC to receive cash from the sales as compensation for cleanup activities that DOE would otherwise have had to pay for out of its appropriated funds. DOE was not itself authorized to keep the proceeds of the sale, nor was it authorized to allow USEC to keep them. DOE may not manipulate the disposition of federal assets to avoid the payment of proceeds for those assets into the federal Treasury.

End Notes

[1] GAO, *Nuclear Material: DOE Has Several Potential Options for Dealing with Depleted Uranium Tails, Each of Which Could Benefit the Government,* GAO-08-606R (Washington, D.C.: Mar. 31, 2008).

[2] According to DOE officials, the objectives of DOE's plan were to: (1) enhance the value and usefulness of DOE's uranium; (2) reduce DOE programmatic costs by decreasing uranium inventories; (3) meet key nonproliferation objectives; and (4) dispose of unmarketable material to facilitate the cleanup of DOE's uranium enrichment plants, in addition to minimizing any material adverse impacts on the domestic uranium industry.

[3] Fluor-B&W Portsmouth LLC is a partnership between Fluor Federal Services, Inc., a subsidiary of Fluor Corporation, an engineering and construction management firm, and Babcock & Wilcox Technical Services Group, a subsidiary of the Babcock & Wilcox Company, a firm that owns and operates large nuclear facilities. Both companies have experience in the handling and disposal of nuclear waste and materials and have worked with DOE to clean up other nuclear weapons facilities across the United States.

[4] H.R. Rep. No. 111-278, at 12 1-22 (2009) (accompanying Energy and Water Development and Related Agencies Appropriations Act, 2010, Pub. L. No. 111-85, 123 Stat. 2845).

[5] USEC Privatization Act, 42 U.S.C. §§ 2297h-2297h-13 (2006); miscellaneous receipts statute, 31 U.S.C. § 3302(b) (2006).

[6] Cold standby is an inactive status that maintains a plant in usable condition so that production at the facility can be restarted in the event of a significant disruption in the nation's supply of enriched uranium.

[7] If constructed, this new plant would enrich uranium by gas centrifuge, a technique that consumes far less energy than the gaseous diffusion process used at DOE's Portsmouth and Paducah facilities.

[8] GAO, *Nuclear Material: DOE's Depleted Uranium Tails Could Be a Source of Revenue for the Government*, GAO-11-752T (Washington, D.C.: June 13, 2011).

[9] We used estimates for future fuel requirements identified by Energy Resources International, Inc., in a market impact analysis it prepared for DOE. See Energy Resources International, Inc., *Quantification of the Potential Impact on Commercial Markets of DOE's Transfer of Natural Uranium Hexafluoride during Calendar Years 2011, 2012, and 2013* (Washington, D.C., December 2010).

[10] Because DOE's first uranium transaction with Fluor-B&W Portsmouth occurred as this report was being finalized, we did not analyze the extent to which DOE's transaction with Fluor-B&W Portsmouth is consistent with federal law. Therefore, this section discusses only the transactions between DOE and USEC.

[11] Miscellaneous receipts statute, 31 U.S.C. § 3302(b) (2006) ("an official or agent of the Government receiving money for the Government from any source shall deposit the money in the Treasury as soon as practicable without deduction for any charge or claim").

[12] 42 U.S.C. §§ 2093, 2201(m) (2006).

[13] We came to the same conclusion when analyzing a similar series of transactions in 2006. See GAO, *Department of Energy: December 2004 Agreement with the United States Enrichment Corporation*, B-3071 37 (Washington, D.C.: July 12, 2006).

[14] The fact that these transactions were sales and not barters is also significant to the question of whether DOE complied with federal fiscal law. By not depositing the proceeds from these sales into the Treasury, DOE violated the miscellaneous receipts statute, as described in greater detail below.

[15] DOE officials have stated that they did not ask, but instead allowed, USEC to solicit buyers or bids for the uranium. In addition, DOE officials approved USEC's valuation of the uranium on the basis of USEC's solicitation of bids. Because parties may assent to an agency relationship by words or actions (*see Restatement (Third) of Agency*, § 1.01 (2006)), whether DOE expressly asked USEC to act as its agent, or merely allowed it to do so and approved the resulting valuation, the result is the same: USEC acted as DOE's agent.

[16] USEC, *U.S. Securities and Exchange Commission, Form 10-K, Annual Report Pursuant to Section 13 or 15(d) of the Securities Exchange Act 1934*, fiscal year ending December 31, 2010.

[17] 42 U.S.C. § 2297h-10 (2006).

[18] Energy Resources International, Inc., *Quantification of the Potential Impact on Commercial Markets of DOE's Transfer of Natural Uranium during the Period October 2009 through December 2013* (Washington, D.C., Nov. 5, 2009).

[19] DOE carried out a sixth transaction with USEC in March 2011. This transfer was not included in Energy Resources International's November 2009 analysis.

[20] Energy Resources International also presented percentage price changes for the spot market, which were based on the firm's estimated price changes in the term market. In other words, the firm estimated a percentage spot price change if the spot market were to experience the same dollar amount of change in price as it had estimated for the term market.

[21] Energy Resources International, Inc., *Quantification of the Potential Impact on Commercial Markets of DOE's Transfer of Natural Uranium Hexafluoride*. This study evaluated the impact on the domestic uranium market of 12 additional transfers totaling up to 4,679

metric tons of natural uranium in the 3-year period from January 2011 through December 2013.

[22] Energy Resources International's expanded analysis of the potential price impact on the spot market, found that DOE's 12 additional planned transfers would have no material adverse impact on uranium producers.

[23] 31 U.S.C. § 3302(b) (2006).

[24] This concept refers to the clause of the Constitution stating, "No Money shall be drawn from the Treasury, but in Consequence of Appropriations made by Law." U.S. Const. art. I, § 9, cl. 7.

[25] GAO, B-307137.

[26] Cummings v. Missouri, 71 U.S. (4 Wall.) 277, 325 (1866).

[27] GAO, *Contractors Collecting Fees at Agency-Hosted* Conferences, B-306663 (Washington, D.C.: Jan. 4, 2006), and GAO, B-307137.

[28] DOE states that we did not refer to or refute the legal conclusions in its internal *Guidance on Barter Transactions Involving DOE-Owned Uranium*, which sets forth the department's position that it has general authority under the Atomic Energy Act to barter uranium for services as it did here. Our report does, however, present DOE's position in this regard. Our report also highlights the fundamental limitation that Congress placed on this general DOE authority: the later and more specific provisions of the USEC Privatization Act, which, as relevant here, authorize only sales of uranium. Because we found that the transactions were sales, we did not consider and did not decide whether barters are also authorized under the USEC Privatization Act. We note, however, that barters are not explicitly or clearly authorized by the terms of the Privatization Act. The provision of the USEC Privatization Act applicable to transactions involving the type of uranium at issue here authorizes only sales, and other provisions draw a distinction between the terms "transfer" and "sell." This distinction suggests that Congress did not intend for sales to encompass barters, which might more easily be understood as a type of transfer, rather than a type of sale. Furthermore, a 2006 bill gave DOE temporary authority to barter uranium, suggesting that Congress did not believe that DOE already had such authority.

[29] *Merriam-Webster's Collegiate Dictionary*, 11th ed. (Springfield, Mass.: 2003).

[30] 42 U.S.C. §§ 2093, 2201(m) (2006).

[31] USEC Privatization Act, 42 U.S.C. §§ 2297h-2297h-13 (2006).

[32] 31 U.S.C. § 3302(b) (2006).

[33] 42 U.S.C. §§ 2093, 2201(m) (2006).

[34] To the extent that the Atomic Energy Act conflicts with the USEC Privatization Act, that conflict should be resolved under the basic tenet of statutory construction that the more specific provision takes precedence. *See, e.g.*, Preiser v. Rodriguez, 411 U.S. 475, 489- 90 (1973). *See also* Watt v. Alaska, 451 U.S. 259, 266-67 (1981); Radzanower v. Touche Ross & Co., 426 U.S. 148, 153 (1976); Morton v. Mancari, 417 U.S. 535, 550-51 (1974); and Smith v. Robinson, 468 U.S. 992 (1984) (Brennan, J., dissenting).

[35] According to DOE, the material provided to USEC was uranium delivered in 1997 and 1998 under the US-Russia Highly Enriched Uranium Purchase Agreement. Public Law Number 105-277, which appropriated the funds for the purchase of this material, specifically provided that this material would become part of DOE's inventory.

[36] The additional conditions are a presidential determination that the material is not needed for national security; a secretarial determination that the sale of the material will not have an adverse material impact on the domestic uranium mining, conversion, and enrichment industries; and that the price paid to the Secretary will not be less than the fair market value of the material. *See* 42 U.S.C. § 2297h-10(d) (2006).

[37] GAO, *Department of Energy: December 2004 Agreement with the United States Enrichment Corporation*, B-307137 (Washington, D.C.: July 12, 2006).

[38] USEC, Inc., *U.S. Securities and Exchange Commission, Form 10-K, Annual Report Pursuant to Section 13 or 15(d) of the Securities Exchange Act of 1934*, fiscal year ending December 31, 2010.

[39] GAO, B-307137 (*citing* Dorf International v. United States, 291 F. Supp. 690, 694 (Cust. Ct. 1968)). *See also* Pier 1 Imports, Inc. v. United States, 708 F. Supp. 351, 354 (Ct. Int'l Trade 1989); Rosenthal-Netter, Inc., v. United States, 679 F. Supp. 21, 23 (Ct. Int'l Trade 1988); and J. C. Penney Purchasing Corp. v. United States, 451 F. Supp. 973, 983 (Cust. Ct. 1978).

[40] 1 *Mechem on the Law of Agency*, §§ 44–48, at 28–32 (2d ed. 1914) (general essence of agency to sell). *See also* Stansifer v. Chrysler Motors Corp. 487 F.2d 59 (9th Cir. 1973); Rosenthal-Netter, 679 F. Supp. at 25; and Pier 1 Imports, 708 F. Supp. at 355 (stressing importance of identifying beneficiary of transaction in determining whether party is agent or principal).

[41] The contract modifications did not provide for delivery of the goods to USEC until after the contract modifications were signed. This fact is not relevant to our analysis, however. Uranium is typically sold through book transfer rather than through physical delivery, so physical possession of the uranium was not necessary for USEC to arrange for its sale. In other words, uranium is fungible. For example, according to USEC officials, USEC did not deliver DOE's uranium to the buyers. Instead, to complete the sales, USEC arranged for book transfer at its Paducah enrichment facility, whereby the buyers received title to an equivalent amount of uranium already located there. Only later did USEC move what had formerly been DOE's uranium to Paducah to replace what it had provided to the buyers out of its other inventories.

[42] We requested but did not receive copies of these sales contracts from USEC. Even assuming the contracts conditioned the sales on the expected receipt of the uranium from DOE, sales were arranged *before* USEC agreed to take the uranium as compensation. Thus, USEC was acting as DOE's agent and not for its own benefit in selling the uranium because it sold the material on DOE's behalf before it accepted the material as part of its "barter" with DOE.

[43] The 10-K states in relevant part, "DOE funded work in 2010 under our contract for maintenance services at the Portsmouth site ('cold shutdown contract') in part through an arrangement whereby DOE transferred to USEC uranium which USEC immediately sold. USEC's receipt of the uranium was not considered a purchase by USEC and no revenue or costs of sales was recorded upon its sale. This is because USEC had no significant risks or rewards of ownership and no potential profit or loss related to the uranium sale. The amount of work provided, and therefore the total value of the contract modification, was dependent on the net value of the uranium realized by USEC upon each sale. Net value of the uranium equaled the cash proceeds from sales less USEC's selling and handling costs. The net value from the uranium sale was recorded as deferred revenue. Revenue was recognized in our contract services segment as cold shutdown services were provided."

[44] It is common for selling agents to be given title and possession to property in order to effect a sale on behalf of the principal. Potts v. Budget Rent-a-Car Sys., No. 04-074, 2005 U.S. Dist. LEXIS 27356, at *13 (N.D. Fla. Nov. 14, 2005) (citing *Restatement (Second) of Agency* § 14N (1958)): independent contractor agents "also fall within the category of trustees, as in the case of a selling agent who has been given title to the subject matter . . . [and] there is an agency [relationship] if in the transaction which they undertake they act for the benefit of another and subject to his control").

[45] The letters indicated that broker fees were applied to sales to certain parties, whereas other sales were made directly to buyers without a broker fee.

[46] 42 U.S.C. § 2297h-10(d)(2)(C) (2006).

[47] When we considered a similar series of transactions between DOE and USEC in 2006, we noted that DOE required USEC to submit a marketing plan for DOE's approval. In the transactions we review in this report, USEC was not required to submit a marketing plan to DOE, but in requesting that USEC value the material, and in approving a value derived from firm offers for the material, DOE effectively did review USEC's marketing strategy.

[48] 1 *Mechem on the Law of Agency*, § 48, at 31 (2nd ed. 1914); *see, e.g.*, Arbuckle v. Kirkpatrick, 98 Tenn. 221, 252-53 (Tenn. 1897).

[49] 31 U.S.C. § 3302(b) (2006).

[50] For a more detailed discussion of the augmentation concept, *see* GAO, *Principles of Federal Appropriations Law*, 3rd ed., vol. II, GAO-06-382SP (Washington, D.C.: February 2006).

[51] *See, e.g.*, Cummings v. Missouri, 71 U.S. (4 Wall.) 277, 325 (1866).

[52] GAO, *Contractors Collecting Fees at Agency-Hosted Conferences*, B-306663 (Washington, D.C.: Jan. 4, 2006), and GAO, B-307137.

[53] *See, e.g.*, Scheduled Airlines Traffic Offices, Inc., v. Department of Defense, 87 F. 3d 1356, 1361-63 (D.C. Cir. 1996) (Defense Department cannot require payment to morale fund of a portion of concession fees derived from unofficial travel); Motor Coach Industries, Inc. v. Dole, 725 F.2d 958, 968 (4th Cir. 1984) (Federal Aviation Administration cannot hold in a trust fund amounts paid by airlines to defray the Aviation Administration's cost of acquiring new shuttle buses for Dulles Airport); GAO, *National Institutes of Health: Food at Government-Sponsored Conferences*, B-300826 (Washington, D.C.: Mar. 3, 2005) (National Institutes of Health cannot authorize its contractor to charge a fee to cover the costs of a formal conference that hosted by the institutes); GAO, *Securities and Exchange Commission: Reduction of Obligation of Appropriated Funds Due to a Sublease*, B-265727 (Washington, D.C.: July 19, 1996) (Securities and Exchange Commission may not reduce its obligation of appropriated funds resulting from a lease and correspondingly increase its available appropriations, by subleasing space and arranging for the sublessee to make its payments directly to the landlord).

[54] GAO, *SBA's Imposition of Oversight Review Fees on PLP Lenders*, B-300248 (Washington, D.C.: Jan. 14, 2004) (in compensating contractors by requiring regulated lenders to pay the contractor's fees, the agency received money for the government because the receipts were to cover government expenses or obligations). *Cf.* GAO, *Return of Proceeds from Diesel Fuel Sales*, B-205901 (Washington, D.C.: May 5, 1982) (money received by the Federal Bureau of Investigation for sales of diesel fuel belonging to a private company as part of an undercover operation was not money for the government and did not have to be deposited into the Treasury).

[55] GAO, *General Services Administration and Real Estate Brokers' Commissions*, B302811 (Washington, D.C.: July 12, 2004), and GAO, *General Services Administration: Real Estate Brokers' Commissions*, B-291947 (Washington, D.C.: Aug. 15, 2003).

[56] As we noted in our 2006 decision with respect to the USEC transactions at issue then, an agency may accept replacement for a damaged item without depositing the value of the replacement item into the Treasury. See GAO, *Bureau of Alcohol, Tobacco, and Firearms: Augmentation of Appropriations: Replacement of Autos by Negligent Third Parties*, 67 Comp. Gen. 510 (Washington, D.C.: July 12, 1988). We concluded in this analysis, as we did in 2006, that this scenario does not constitute an in-kind replacement of damaged items. Rather, DOE is seeking to pay for new services—the accelerated cleanup of the Portsmouth Gaseous Diffusion Plant—not to replace or repair federal property.

INDEX

A

access, 51, 52, 71, 88
accessibility, 33
accounting, 86
acid, 25, 35, 53, 54, 55
agencies, vii, 1, 2, 3, 5, 6, 11, 13, 16, 22, 25, 28, 29, 30, 31, 33, 36, 37, 38, 39, 42, 43, 48, 59, 64, 93
Alaska, 102
anxiety, 74
appropriations, 82, 98, 104
Appropriations Act, 65, 100
arsenic, vii, 4, 7, 8
assessment, 12, 13, 16, 19, 41, 57, 65
assets, 56, 76, 81, 82, 83, 84, 92, 93, 94, 95, 97, 100
audit, 6, 44, 66, 86
authorities, 2, 19
authority, 11, 12, 13, 15, 75, 80, 82, 93, 94, 99, 102

B

bankruptcy, 54
barriers, 54, 55
barter, 80, 81, 82, 84, 92, 95, 96, 97, 102, 103
base, 58
bicarbonate, 8
blends, 73
bonding, 17, 57, 58
bonds, 56
Bureau of Indian Affairs, 56, 59
Bureau of Land Management, 2, 3, 5, 37, 39, 48, 49, 50, 51, 54, 56
buyer, 94, 97
buyers, 67, 76, 95, 97, 98, 101, 103
by-products, 7

C

cancer, 68
carbon, 8, 64
carbon dioxide, 8, 64
cash, 65, 76, 77, 80, 81, 82, 83, 84, 93, 95, 97, 99, 100, 103
category a, 33, 35
cattle, 48
cheese, 87
chemical, 7, 56, 62, 68
chemicals, 54, 57, 68, 88
Clean Water Act, 12
cleaning, 32, 43, 59
cleanup, vii, viii, 1, 3, 5, 6, 13, 29, 30, 31, 33, 34, 37, 39, 42, 43, 48, 49, 50, 51, 52, 53, 54, 55, 56, 59, 60, 61, 62, 65, 68, 70, 73, 76, 78, 80, 81, 82, 83, 84, 85, 86, 90, 92, 94, 95, 97, 99, 100, 104
climate, 54

coal, 56, 79, 87
commercial, 62, 64, 65, 66, 70, 73, 74, 86
commodity, 29, 31, 32, 39, 46, 47, 57, 59, 67, 77, 97
commodity markets, 67
compensation, 76, 83, 99, 100, 103
compliance, 16, 17
Comprehensive Environmental Response, Compensation, and Liability Act (CERCLA), 3, 13
conference, 65, 104
conflict, 102
congress, 57, 62, 63, 75, 78, 80, 81, 93, 98, 102
consent, 43
constitution, 63, 81, 102
construction, 58, 100, 102
contaminated sites, 13, 43
contaminated soil, 35, 53
contaminated water, 35
contamination, 8, 13, 33, 43, 53, 56, 59
control measures, 53
conversations, 41
cooling, 68
cooperation, 5, 27
coordination, 5, 13, 27, 36, 37, 38
copper, 56, 79
cost, 2, 3, 8, 13, 14, 16, 17, 18, 19, 25, 27, 28, 29, 32, 33, 35, 37, 43, 48, 49, 50, 51, 52, 53, 54, 55, 57, 59, 69, 84, 87, 99, 104
costs of production, 84
covering, 21, 55, 57, 77
credentials, 71
crystals, 89
customers, 67, 88, 89
cycles, 27

D

data collection, 37
database, 5, 17, 20, 30, 31, 32, 36, 38, 39, 40, 41, 45, 46, 47, 58, 59
decay, 7
decontamination, 62, 65, 68
deduction, 80, 98, 101

deficiencies, 17
degradation, 11
delegates, 11
demand characteristic, 78
Department of Agriculture, 5, 38
Department of Defense, 78, 104
Department of Energy, viii, 2, 3, 5, 38, 39, 44, 61, 63, 64, 85, 88, 90, 91, 101, 102
Department of Justice, 59
Department of the Interior, 5, 38
Department of the Treasury, 56
deposits, 7, 8, 12, 13, 39, 42, 57, 87, 89
depth, 8
diesel fuel, 104
diffusion, 86, 90, 91, 101
diffusion process, 101
disposition, 65, 70, 73, 84, 92, 93, 100
domestic demand, 7
draft, 12, 15, 32, 38, 59, 82, 83, 84
drainage, 35, 50, 53, 54, 55
drinking water, 12

E

educational institutions, 93
electricity, 64
employees, 71, 98
employment, 84
energy, viii, 61, 64, 66, 78, 79, 91, 101
engineering, 100
environment, vii, 1, 4, 7, 12, 13, 43, 57
environmental control, 7
environmental effects, 13
environmental impact, 11, 13, 24, 56, 59
environmental impact statement, 13, 24
Environmental Protection Agency (EPA), 2, 3, 5, 6, 11, 12, 28, 30, 31, 32, 35, 38, 39, 42, 47, 53, 55, 56, 57, 59, 68
environmental quality, 5
environmental regulations, 16
environmental standards, 5
equipment, 15, 27, 33, 49, 51, 68, 91
erosion, 4, 7, 16, 50, 53, 54
evidence, 6, 44, 66, 82, 83, 86
exercise, 76, 94, 96

expertise, 27, 28, 36, 77
explosives, 88
exposure, 98
extraction, vii, 1, 2, 4, 5, 7, 8, 12, 14, 15, 16, 19, 21, 22, 24, 29, 30, 32, 39, 40, 46, 57, 58, 60
extraction operations, vii, 1, 5, 14, 19, 39
extracts, 8, 87

F

fabrication, 57, 66, 92
fear, 72, 75, 81
federal agency, 23, 48, 49, 50, 51, 52, 53, 54, 55, 80, 98, 99
Federal Bureau of Investigation, 104
federal government, 4, 19, 20, 22, 58, 59, 67, 76, 82, 95
federal land, vii, 1, 2, 3, 4, 5, 6, 11, 13, 14, 19, 20, 25, 29, 30, 32, 36, 37, 39, 42, 44, 47, 56, 57, 59
federal law, viii, 39, 62, 65, 66, 86, 92, 101
federal regulations, 15
fencing, 53
financial, vii, 1, 2, 4, 5, 6, 11, 13, 14, 16, 17, 19, 20, 24, 25, 26, 27, 28, 29, 32, 36, 37, 38, 39, 40, 41, 42, 45, 56, 57, 58, 76, 99
financial resources, 56
fisheries, 4
fission, 64
flexibility, 17
fluid, 7, 13
funds, 31, 32, 35, 59, 67, 80, 81, 83, 97, 98, 99, 100, 102, 104

G

GAO, vii, viii, 1, 2, 3, 16, 18, 22, 23, 32, 33, 39, 45, 47, 55, 56, 58, 59, 61, 62, 63, 69, 70, 73, 74, 83, 88, 92, 100, 101, 102, 103, 104
General Services Administration, 99, 104
geology, 8
grades, 19

grasslands, 11
grazing, 48
groundwater, 8, 12, 13, 27, 28, 53, 55, 57, 58, 89
grouping, 30
guidance, 5, 14, 15, 17, 19, 22, 25, 37, 39, 57, 85

H

habitat, 4
hazardous materials, 62, 68
hazardous substances, 56, 59
hazards, vii, 4, 6, 31, 33, 34, 35, 43, 48, 49, 50, 51, 52, 53, 54, 55, 59
health, vii, 4, 8, 54, 56, 59
heavy metals, vii, 4, 7, 8, 54
hiking trails, 35
house, 1, 4, 64
House of Representatives, 1, 4, 64
human, 7, 35, 43, 51
human health, 7, 35, 43, 51

I

imports, 7
improvements, 59
Indian reservation, 35
individuals, 56
industries, 63, 72, 78, 102
industry, viii, 8, 39, 61, 62, 64, 65, 66, 67, 72, 74, 78, 80, 84, 86, 87, 99, 100
information sharing, 37
information technology, 39
infrastructure, 7
inspections, 12, 29, 31, 69
interagency coordination, 27
investment, 75, 78
isotope, 64, 66, 91
issues, 25, 39, 41, 59, 76

J

Japan, 79

L

laws, 5, 11, 31, 56, 59, 66
leaching, 57, 88
lead, 15, 56, 59
livestock, 52

M

magnesium, 56
majority, 2, 8, 15
management, vii, viii, 5, 15, 22, 37, 61, 62, 65, 66, 69, 70, 71, 72, 74, 75, 77, 80, 81, 82, 84, 85, 86, 92, 97, 100
manufacturing, 70
marketing, 81, 103
marketing strategy, 103
materials, 4, 7, 13, 35, 48, 49, 50, 51, 52, 54, 56, 59, 63, 76, 77, 85, 100
matter, 103
membranes, 91
memorandums of understanding, 5, 39
metals, 8
methodology, 6, 66
Mexico, 7, 12, 31, 39, 40, 52, 57, 59
migration, 55
mission, 31
Missouri, 102, 104
modifications, 76, 82, 83, 85, 95, 96, 103
Montana, 35, 52, 59
morale, 104
motivation, 97

N

National Forest System, 11, 57
National Institutes of Health, 104
National Park Service, 6, 30, 31, 32, 33, 34, 35, 42, 47, 48, 49, 50, 55, 59
national security, 63, 77, 86, 102
natural disaster, 79
negotiating, 86, 97
negotiation, 15

Nuclear Regulatory Commission (NRC), 2, 3, 5, 11, 12, 13, 24, 25, 26, 27, 28, 36, 37, 38, 39, 45, 56, 59, 90, 92
nuclear weapons, viii, 7, 61, 64, 67, 70, 78, 90, 100
nuclear weapons production, viii, 61

O

oil, 56, 79
operations, vii, 1, 2, 4, 5, 6, 7, 8, 11, 12, 13, 14, 15, 16, 17, 18, 19, 20, 21, 22, 23, 24, 25, 26, 27, 28, 36, 37, 39, 40, 41, 43, 44, 45, 51, 56, 57, 58, 59, 64, 71, 86
oversight, vii, 1, 2, 5, 11, 14, 26, 36, 37, 39, 65
ownership, 67, 85, 86, 103

P

participants, 79
permit, 13, 57, 98
plants, 64, 71, 100
plutonium, 73
pollutants, 12
polychlorinated biphenyl, 68
polyurethane, 48, 49, 50, 51, 52
polyurethane foam, 48, 49, 50, 51, 52
ponds, 53, 54
power generation, 7
power plants, 57, 64, 67, 86
preparation, 27
president, 77
price changes, 101
privatization, 93
producers, 78, 81, 102
profit, 67, 76, 94, 95, 103
project, 13, 19, 84
proposition, 98
protection, 13
public domain, 5, 12
public health, 12, 57

R

radiation, 13, 54
radioactive contamination, 13, 35
radium, vii, 4, 7
radon, 7
rainfall, 53
real estate, 99
recall, 95
recommendations, 2, 38
recovery, 3, 5, 44, 89
recycling, 68
regulations, vii, 1, 5, 11, 13, 14, 15, 17, 18, 26, 31, 39, 56, 57
regulatory oversight, 38
rehabilitation, 4
reimburse, 59
relevance, 22
reliability, 6, 39, 41, 42
remediation, 5, 33, 35, 38, 43, 48, 49, 50, 51, 52, 53, 54, 55, 56, 59
rent, 20
repair, 52, 104
requirements, 11, 13, 15, 16, 36, 62, 63, 65, 71, 72, 73, 86, 101
resale, 97
reserves, 57
resins, 8
resources, 11, 13, 14, 15, 16, 27, 31, 79
response, 59
restoration, 8, 27, 28
revenue, 103
rewards, 103
risk, 7, 8, 35, 76, 82, 83, 95
risks, 54, 97, 103
rods, 92
royalty, 12, 57, 58
rules, 11
runoff, 4, 52, 53
Russia, 7, 93, 102

S

safety, vii, 4, 6, 12, 31, 33, 34, 43, 48, 49, 50, 51, 52, 53, 54, 55, 57, 59
scope, 6, 41, 42, 66
Securities Exchange Act, 101, 103
sediment, 53, 54, 55
selenium, vii, 4, 8
sellers, 67
senate, 64
services, 39, 62, 65, 67, 68, 70, 76, 84, 85, 86, 92, 94, 95, 97, 99, 100, 102, 103, 104
signs, 48, 49, 52
silver, 56
sludge, 55
sodium, 8
South Dakota, 40, 45, 53, 59
specifications, 41, 70
spot market, 67, 78, 79, 96, 101, 102
stability, 52
stakeholders, 65
state, 5, 11, 12, 13, 15, 17, 18, 19, 26, 27, 28, 30, 35, 36, 39, 42, 43, 44, 46, 57, 58, 59, 87, 93
state authorities, 87
states, 5, 7, 11, 12, 13, 17, 19, 21, 30, 31, 39, 40, 42, 43, 57, 59, 62, 68, 70, 80, 95, 102, 103
statutes, 66
statutory authority, 98
steel, 49, 57
storage, 69, 71
structure, 52, 77, 95, 97
superfund, 13, 59
surplus, viii, 61, 63, 73

T

target, viii, 61, 62, 71, 72, 74
technical comments, 2, 38
techniques, 66
technology, 91
Tennessee Valley Authority, 71, 73, 78
time frame, 17, 25, 28, 85

tracks, 32, 58, 85
trade, 66, 84, 86
transaction costs, 69, 70, 76, 77, 96, 97
transactions, viii, 22, 61, 62, 63, 65, 67, 68, 69, 71, 73, 75, 76, 77, 78, 80, 81, 82, 83, 85, 86, 92, 93, 94, 95, 97, 98, 99, 101, 102, 103, 104
transparency, 65
transport, 52
treasury, 63, 75, 77, 79, 80, 81, 82, 83, 84, 93, 95, 97, 98, 99, 100, 101, 102, 104
treatment, 12, 35, 55, 56, 59
tribal lands, 56, 59
trust fund, 13, 104

U

U.S. Army Corps of Engineers, 59
U.S. Geological Survey (USGS), 3, 8, 42, 46, 57, 59, 87
Ukraine, 73
united, v, vii, 1, 4, 7, 11, 12, 58, 61, 62, 63, 64, 66, 67, 85, 90, 99, 100, 101, 102, 103
United States, v, vii, 1, 4, 7, 11, 12, 58, 61, 62, 63, 64, 66, 67, 85, 90, 99, 100, 101, 102, 103
updating, 75
uranium enrichment facility, viii, 61, 64
uranium exploration, vii, 1, 2, 4, 5, 14, 23, 39, 79
uranium industry officials, viii, 62, 72, 74
uranium market analysts, viii, 62
uranium mining, vii, 1, 4, 5, 7, 37, 38, 41, 43, 56, 57, 59, 63, 72, 78, 87, 102

uranium operations, vii, 1, 2, 5, 6, 11, 13, 15, 20, 21, 23, 24, 26, 28, 36, 39, 40, 41, 42, 43, 44, 56, 58, 59

V

valuation, 76, 77, 78, 83, 85, 96, 97, 101
vanadium, 12, 19, 20, 57, 79
varieties, 56
vegetation, 52, 54, 55
ventilation, 50, 51

W

Washington, 35, 40, 54, 56, 57, 58, 59, 66, 100, 101, 102, 104
waste, vii, 4, 7, 8, 30, 34, 35, 48, 49, 50, 51, 52, 53, 54, 55, 56, 100
water, 4, 7, 8, 28, 35, 43, 52, 53, 54, 55, 56, 68, 89
water supplies, 52
weapons, viii, 61, 64, 66, 78
web, 5, 40
wells, 3, 8, 13, 28, 53
wetlands, 53
wildlife, 4, 52
wood, 48, 49, 50

Z

zinc, 56